THE MISSING INGREDIENT
to success

Michael Cameneti

THE MISSING INGREDIENT
to success

Michael Cameneti

First Printing 2004

ISBN 0-89276-971-8

In the U.S. write:
Kenneth Hagin Ministries
P.O. Box 50126
Tulsa, OK 74150-0126
1-888-28-FAITH
www.rhema.org

In Canada write:
Kenneth Hagin Ministries
P.O. Box 335, Station D
Etobicoke (Toronto), Ontario
Canada, M9A 4X3

CONTENTS

Introduction

T he title of this book is *The Missing Ingredient to Success.* You may be thinking to yourself, *Do you mean there could be a missing ingredient in my life? And if I add this one ingredient, would it help me become successful?* The answer to both of these questions is *yes.*

This missing ingredient is probably not at all what you think it is; nevertheless, it is absolutely necessary if you want to enjoy success and receive the promises of God in every area of life. In fact, although prosperity isn't the subject of this book, this message may be the most important teaching on prosperity you'll ever read.

The missing ingredient to success is found in Romans 3:18: *"There is no fear of God before their eyes."* This book could have been called *The Fear of the Lord.*

Instead, I chose to give it a title that puts the emphasis on the end result of fearing God rather than on the act of fearing Him. I realize that people often tend to tune out a teaching on this subject because they don't understand what the fear of God is or the benefits that result from fearing Him.

Most of us have heard people say, "God's going to get you," or we have read our insurance policies that refer to natural disasters as "acts of God." Unfortunately, phrases like these give people, including Christians, the wrong idea about God.

I pray this book will help you realize that fearing God doesn't mean you live in terror of Him or of what He may do to you. God is *not* out to get you! In fact, there is great benefit in fearing God, for He loves you and wants to bless you. My desire is to show you how this one missing ingredient—walking in the fear of God—will open your life to His blessings and His love more than anything else you can do.

I approached this subject a little differently so you would be able to see that fearing God is a *good* thing. When you fear Him, you please Him; and when you please Him, He opens up the windows of Heaven and enables you to achieve spiritual and natural success in every area of your life.

Michael Cameneti

CHAPTER ONE

What Does the Fear of the Lord Accomplish in Our Lives?

M any Christians are frustrated because they're not experiencing the kind of success the Bible says they should have. They seem to be doing all the right things. They listen to teachings; they confess scriptures; they believe God's Word; they take authority over the devil. But still they struggle to receive healing, have their needs met, or achieve success in their jobs, careers, and relationships.

Why are so many Christians failing to experience the victory that is rightfully theirs? A primary reason is that they are missing a very important ingredient in their lives: *the fear of God.*

Too often ministers shy away from teaching on the fear of God because they are afraid it will make people uncomfortable. Certainly it isn't always a popular subject to teach. But although this isn't the type of message that makes people want to shout and dance when they hear it, the fear of God is an essential part of the Christian life.

In fact, this message is so important that Ecclesiastes 12:13 reads, *"Let us hear the conclusion of the whole matter: FEAR GOD, and keep his command-ments: for this is the whole duty of man."* Solomon, the author of Ecclesiastes and the wisest man who ever lived, wrote this book near the end of his life. After reflecting back on his life, Solomon came to the conclu-sion that the purpose of man's existence can be summed up in just two words: *Fear God.*

Our 'Limiter'

Did you know that the fear of God acts like a "lim-iter" in our lives? Consider the many things in the physical world that have limiters on them. Vehicles are good exam-ples. When many of us were younger, we rode minibikes or go-carts, both of which had limiters on them. Limiters are put on these kinds of motorized vehicles to prevent them from performing at their full potential.

Car manufacturers build cars to shut down after they reach a certain speed, usually 100 or 120 miles per hour. These cars have the potential of going much faster, but when they reach a predetermined speed, a computer chip in the cars "tells" them to shut down. The driver may think the car is out of gas because it will start sput-tering and eventually come to a stop. But that computer chip is the true limiter, for it prevents the car from exceeding a certain speed.

Another great example is lasers. A laser can burn through brick walls, metal, and just about anything else—yet today laser surgery has become commonplace. So how can a laser be used on a person's body without damaging it? The answer is a limiter, which prevents the laser from operating at its full potential.

Similarly, there are limiters in your life that will not allow you to operate at *your* full potential. Some of these limiters can be detrimental, holding you back from worshipping God or from experiencing His blessings on your finances, your health, your mental wellness, or any other area of your life.

For example, people who suffered through an abusive childhood may have a poor self-image that keeps them from believing they can ever be successful in life. If this type of attitude isn't dealt with, it will act as a limiter on their potential for success throughout their lives.

On the other hand, limiters can be beneficial in some areas. For example, it is good to have a limiter on your tongue so you don't always say the things you want to say. Limiters that prevent you from being unfaithful to your spouse, stealing from your employer, or cheating on your taxes are also very good!

The Word of God teaches that without a limiter in our lives, we will live any way we want to live. That's why God specifically gave us a tool that enables us to live the life *He* wants us to live.

The Fruit of Not Fearing the Lord:
A Life Without a Limiter

In Romans 3, the Bible describes people who have no limiters in their lives.

ROMANS 3:9–18

9 What then? are we better than they? No, in no wise: for we have before proved both Jews and Gentiles, that they are all under sin;

10 As it is written, There is none righteous, no, not one:

11 There is none that understandeth, there is none that seeketh after God.

12 They are all gone out of the way, they are together become unprofitable; there is none that doeth good, no, not one.

13 Their throat is an open sepulchre; with their tongues they have used deceit; the poison of asps is under their lips:

14 Whose mouth is full of cursing and bitterness:

15 Their feet are swift to shed blood:

16 Destruction and misery are in their ways:

17 And the way of peace have they not known:

18 There is no fear of God before their eyes.

People who lack limiters are unprofitable in life (v. 12) because they don't know the right way and they live undisciplined lives. These people don't have their tongues under control, and they seek only to please themselves. Unfortunately, the end result of a life without limiters is a life without God. Or in the case of those who are born again, the end result is a life of lukewarm Christianity, without the peace or the success God intends for each of His children to enjoy.

Sadly, we all know Christians like this. We can usually tell just by looking at them that they don't have peace and are not living profitable lives. They have veered off the right path and are now living a life that leads to destruction.

What does God want to do with these Christians? Does He desire to destroy them? Absolutely not! He loves them and wants to use them for His glory. But in order for His purposes to come to pass in their lives, these Christians will have to change. How? By learning to embrace the limiter that is required for living a holy life. That limiter is the fear of God.

Let's look again at what Romans 3:18 tells us: *"There is no fear of God before their eyes."* Notice that the fear of the Lord is to be kept *before your eyes*. What happens if you *don't* keep it before your eyes? Just go back and read Romans 3:12–17, and you'll discover the answer.

Unfortunately, there are far too many Christians who live their lives within these verses. Verse 18 tells us why: *They have no fear of God before their eyes.* This is true for Christians and non-Christians alike. The bad things described in this passage of Scripture will happen in the life of every person who fails to walk in the fear of God.

It is the fear of God that keeps a limiter on you and prevents you from living as the world lives. This is essential for your spiritual walk, for God has called you to be an imitator of Him, *not* the world (Eph. 5:1). When this limiter is effectively operating in your life, you won't cheat the government; you won't cheat on your spouse; you won't cheat in *any* area of life. Why? Because the fear of the Lord drives and compels you to walk in integrity, no matter what.

Dishonesty and the Fear of Man

Let's talk about some of the negative results that occur when a person fails to keep the fear of God in front of his eyes. Two of these results are *dishonesty* and *the fear of man*. We can find an excellent biblical example of these two characteristics in Genesis 20, where Abraham meets Abimelech. Verse 2 reads, *"And Abraham said of Sarah his wife, She is my sister: and Abimelech king of Gerar sent, and took Sarah."*

When Abimelech asked Abraham about Sarah, Abraham told him that she was his sister! According to the Bible, Abraham lied because he was afraid (v. 11). Afraid of whom? Certainly Abraham wasn't afraid of God, or he wouldn't have lied! If Abraham had been walking in the fear of the Lord at that moment, he would have said, "This is my wife, and we serve the only true God"—and no one would have been able to lay a hand on either of them. But instead, Abraham let the fear of God fall from before his eyes. As a result, he was caught in a lie because he feared man more than God.

Flattery

Just as Romans 3:9-18 talks about people who don't keep the fear of God before their eyes, so does Psalm 36:1-3. However, the passage in Psalms shows us a different end result.

> PSALM 36:1-3
> 1   The transgression of the wicked saith within my heart, that there is no fear of God before his eyes.
> 2   For he flattereth himself in his own eyes, until his iniquity be found to be hateful.
> 3   The words of his mouth are iniquity and deceit: he hath left off to be wise, and to do good.

Notice the message of verse 2: The person who doesn't keep the fear of God before his eyes begins to *flatter himself in his own eyes.*

Flattery is actually perverted praise. It occurs when we tell someone what he or she wants to hear, but it isn't what we really believe or feel.

We all know people who will say one thing when they're with one crowd and then say something else when they're with a different crowd. For example, they might tell a person that they like his new outfit. But then they'll walk away and tell someone else how ugly they think that person's outfit is! People who do that are using flattery for their own selfish purposes because they have failed to keep the fear of God before their eyes.

Flattery is extremely prevalent in our society today. People tell you what you want to hear so you'll feel good about yourself, even when they don't believe their own words. Often they will use flattery just to avoid telling the truth.

But God will never flatter you. He will always "tell it like it is," even when it isn't what you want to hear.

This issue often comes up between husbands and wives. Unfortunately, many women in our society condition their husbands to flatter them. Wives will put on a new dress and then ask their husbands how they look. However, a wife doesn't always want to hear her husband's honest opinion; she just wants to hear that she looks great, whether her husband thinks so or not!

One of the principles my wife and I established early in our marriage was that she would never set me up to flatter her and that I would always be honest. In return, I would encourage and compliment her on my own so she would never have to put me in an awkward position. Thus, when my wife asks me if I like something, she is prepared for an honest response. She understands the concept, "Don't ask if you don't want to know!"

Speaking the truth in love (Eph. 4:15) may not always be the easiest or the most popular thing to do, but if you fear God, you will do it anyway. It may even hurt or offend the person at first. But in the long run, he or she will appreciate your honesty, and you will maintain integrity in your Christian walk. The key, however, is to speak the truth *in love*!

Desensitization to Sin

Along with flattery, dishonesty, and the fear of man, another result of not fearing God is *desensitization to sin*.

If you've been saved for a number of years, you may remember a time in your Christian walk when your conscience was more repulsed by sinful things than it is now. Early on in your walk with the Lord, there were probably certain things that you just wouldn't do. For instance, you may have determined not to watch a movie that had nudity in it. If you ever encountered such a scene in the movie you were watching, you'd blush and think, *This is wrong. I'm a Christian, and I shouldn't be watching this!* Then you would either get up and leave the theater or turn off the television.

But as life goes on and you live in this world as a Christian for a while, it is easy to become less and less sensitive to sin if you're not careful. Soon you might find yourself watching television shows and movies that have sin and perversion in them, and you won't even bat an eye! At that point, you need to realize that you have become desensitized and have ceased to keep the fear of God before your eyes.

It's important that you don't allow your heart to become desensitized to the point where you can do wrong without even feeling badly about it. But did you know that it isn't enough just to feel badly after you do something wrong? The key is to be convicted and constrained not to yield to the temptation before you ever act on it. That's the way to avoid the sin altogether!

This is where the fear of the Lord comes in. It will stop you before you ever do wrong instead of simply convicting you after you have committed the deed.

Once the pleasure of sin is past, most people feel badly and wish they had never committed the sin. This is a good thing, for sorrow over committed sin often leads people to repentance. However, it is even better for people to live with the fear of the Lord before their eyes, because then they won't participate in sin to begin with!

Unanswered Prayer

Another result of not fearing God is *unanswered prayer*, as revealed in Proverbs 1.

PROVERBS 1:28–33
28 Then shall they call upon me, but I will not answer; they shall seek me early, but they shall not find me:
29 For that they hated knowledge, and did not choose the fear of the Lord:

30 They would none of my counsel: they despised
all my reproof.
31 Therefore shall they eat of the fruit of their own
way, and be filled with their own devices.
32 For the turning away of the simple shall slay
them, and the prosperity of fools shall destroy
them.
33 But whoso hearkeneth unto me shall dwell safely,
and shall be quiet from fear of evil.

The people who are described in this passage of
Scripture don't walk in the fear of the Lord. We know
this because verses 29 and 30 say that these people hate
knowledge; they reject God's wisdom, counsel, and correction; and they are disobedient to His commands.

Notice the end result of these people's choice *not* to
fear God: They call on Him and they seek Him, but they
fail to receive any response from Him (v. 28).

This shows again how important the fear of the Lord
is to our success. How can we ever be successful in any
endeavor we undertake if God doesn't answer when we
call on Him and we can't find Him when we seek Him?
The truth is, we cannot. If we choose to forsake the fear of
God, we are on our own in life, relegated to making deci-
sions and going through the trials of life without His help.

Choose to Fear the Lord

We've seen that we have to keep the fear of the
Lord before our eyes, but Proverbs 1:29 tells us that
fearing God is a *choice*. How often will we have to make

that choice? Proverbs 23:17 tells us: *". . . Be thou in the fear of the Lord ALL THE DAY LONG."*

How often must we choose to fear God? The answer is *all day, every day.* In fact, we have to choose to keep the fear of the Lord before our eyes several times throughout the day as we face different circumstances. The reason is simple: If we don't fear God, we will sin.

For example, perhaps you're a businessperson who travels a lot and therefore spends a significant amount of time away from home and from your spouse. In that case, you probably face many opportunities to let the fear of God drop from before your eyes and yield to temptations that you would normally resist when at home. But every moment of every day, you have a choice to either fear God or to live like you want to live. Choosing to walk in the fear of the Lord will enable you to live behind closed doors the way you live when others are watching.

According to Proverbs 1:31, some people are eating the fruit of their own way, and it has nothing to do with what they're confessing or whether or not they're tithing, praying, or fasting. Many times ministers give people formulas to follow: "If you do this and that, you will get such-and-such result." Well, here is *God's* formula: *"Fear Me, or you will eat the fruit of your own way."*

Verse 31 goes on to say that those who don't fear God will *". . . be filled with their own devices."* In the Hebrew, it says they will be filled with their own _purposes._ In other words, they live their lives doing things their own way.

This is how it works: The person described in Proverbs 1:31—who is eating the fruit of his own way and is filled with his own purposes—gets an idea that he thinks will lead to financial prosperity. He pursues that idea, but the outcome is failure. As the person looks for someone besides himself to blame for his problems, he begins to think, _The preachers say that all I have to do is tithe. I've been doing that—and giving offerings too! So why am I not seeing prosperity?_

But biblical financial prosperity won't come to a person who is filled with his own ways and doesn't fear God. Proverbs 1:32 explains why: _". . . The prosperity of fools shall destroy them."_ The prosperity of fools comes to those who do things their own way—in other words, those who don't fear God and won't receive His reproof or correction. This kind of prosperity destroys people. It is _not_ a blessing!

You can't override your disobedience just by giving—you have to be obedient to the Word in other areas as well. It isn't enough to give an offering when you're not walking in the fear of God. You won't be blessed with God's blessings if you don't fear the Lord.

Instead of doing things your way, you should want to do what _God_ wants and to please Him in all your ways. The Bible gives you a precious promise when you choose to live your life in this manner.

PROVERBS 3:5,6

5 Trust in the Lord with all thine heart; and lean
not unto thine own understanding.

6 In all thy ways acknowledge him, and he shall
direct thy paths.

As you acknowledge God in everything you do—as
you walk in reverential fear of Him—He promises to
direct your paths.

The Fruit of Fearing the Lord

Proverbs 1:33 says that if you listen to God's voice,
you will *". . . dwell safely, and shall be quiet from fear
of evil."* When you fear God, you will fear nothing else.
You will not fear losing your job. You will not fear
where your money is coming from or how you're going
to make ends meet. You will not worry and fret about
the possibility of sickness and disease attacking your
family. You will not fear *anything.*

When you have the fear of the Lord in your life, you
will not let cursing come out of your mouth. You will not
turn from God and walk down the wrong path. You will
not be a person whose ways are destructive or whose life
is unprofitable. Instead, you will walk down the right
path and be a valuable asset to the Kingdom of God.

In addition, fearing God will bring you prosperity.
You may be thinking, *How on earth could the fear of the
Lord tie in with my money?* First, you need to under-
stand that prosperity is not only about money. It's about

enjoying success in _every_ area of your life. When the Bible talks about prosperity, it is actually talking about being successful, and the key to being successful is to fear the Lord. In fact, if you walk in this area of the Word, you'll find that you'll never have to go after money. Instead, money will come after you!

Consider your job, for instance. If you are unprofitable on your job, your boss won't want to keep you around very long. But as you consistently walk in the fear of God, He will cause you to become so profitable so that your boss will begin to think, _I'm glad I have that person working for me. He's a great asset to this company!_ And it won't just be your boss who thinks that way. All those who get to know you will wish you were working for _them_!

Never forget, however, that all these blessings come as a result of a deliberate choice. Day by day and moment by moment, you must choose to fear the Lord instead of walking in your own ways. Only then will you know what it is to live in God's abundance as you begin to eat the fruit of _His_ ways!

CHAPTER TWO

What Is the Fear of the Lord?

T he first step in understanding the fear of the Lord is
to define it. There are many passages in the Bible
that tell us exactly what it means to fear God. For
example, Proverbs 8:13 gives us one definition: *"The
fear of the Lord is to hate evil: pride, and arrogancy, and
the evil way, and the froward mouth, do I hate."*

If you read this verse in context, you will find that
wisdom is speaking, revealing to us that the fear of the
Lord means to *hate evil*, which means to hate anything
that is sinful or wrong. You could say it this way: *The
fear of the Lord is to dislike or disapprove of whatever
God dislikes or disapproves of.*

With this understanding, we can go back to
Proverbs 8:13 and insert the word "hate" in front of
each of the sins listed. In other words, to walk in the

fear of the Lord is to hate evil, to hate pride, to hate arrogancy, to hate the evil way, and to hate the froward mouth.

Job 28:28 gives us further insight into what it means to fear the Lord: *"And unto man he said, Behold, the fear of the Lord, that is wisdom; and to depart from evil is understanding."* We're now beginning to get a clearer picture of this subject. First, we learned that to fear God is to hate evil and sin; now we see that the fear of the Lord is *wisdom.* So if we acquire wisdom from the Word and we hate what is evil, we will be on our way to fearing God.

A Definition
That Could Change Your Life!

There is a definition from the Hebrew language that would absolutely change our lives if we got a revelation of it. I believe it's the best definition of the fear of God that I've ever read. It's from *Vine's Complete Expository Dictionary of Old and New Testament Words*, and it says that the fear of the Lord is ". . . not a mere 'fear' of His power and righteous retribution, but a wholesome dread of displeasing Him."[1]

The first part of this definition addresses a misconception many people have by telling us what the fear of the Lord is *not*. People mistakenly think that to fear God means to live in terror of Him. But that's wrong! God loves us and cares for us. He would never do anything to harm us.

The second part of the definition tells us what the fear of the Lord *is*: a wholesome dread within us of ever displeasing God.

The key here is the origin of that dread. It comes not from a fear of what God might do to us, but from an understanding of how much He loves us. When we truly begin to understand how great God's love is toward us, we'll never want to do anything that would cause Him to be disappointed in us.

You've probably had relationships with people—parents, teachers, coaches—who cared about you very much and for whom you had a great deal of respect. Chances are that you always tried to please them and never wanted to let them down. Why is that? Because you recognized how much these individuals loved you, and you knew that if you ever did something wrong, they might be disappointed in you. You never feared the prospect of being harmed or punished by them. Instead, you feared the prospect of failing them or letting them down.

That is the way it is supposed to be in your relationship with God. When you fear Him, you want to avoid all sin—not because you're afraid He might hurt you if you do something wrong, but because you don't ever want to do anything that would displease Him. Your understanding of how deeply God loves and cares for you compels you to willingly do all that He asks of you.

The Fear of the Lord
In Our Everyday Lives

So how does the fear of God affect our everyday lives? When we choose to fear the Lord, we choose not to do anything that would displease our Heavenly Father. In fact, we dread even the thought of displeasing Him. Our goal becomes to please Him in everything we do.

This is why the fear of God is such a crucial ingredient to success in life. In fact, I believe most people become depressed because they are *not* walking in the fear of God. They yield to sin in certain areas and therefore live lives that are displeasing to God. Yet they feel badly about what they are doing, and that opens the door for depression to set in.

Think about it. If you know you are pleasing your Father, what can possibly depress you? When you're pleasing God, you know you're doing exactly what He created you to do, and that causes you to have joy.

Now let's see how fearing the Lord brings God's power into some practical areas of our lives. Consider first what happens when a child gets a revelation of what it means to fear God. He now wants to please God and to do what the Bible says, and one of the main things the Bible tells a child to do is to honor his parents. So even if this particular child happens to get upset with his parents one day, he won't rebel against them because he fears God.

Do you see the power that is resident in a person's life as he walks in the fear of God? In the child's case, the power begins to operate when he thinks, *I don't want to displease God. I'm not going to obey my parents just to make them feel good. I'm going to obey them because I have a Father in Heaven whom I want to please.*

I can use myself as an example. As I was growing up, I was like most kids in that I always wanted to please my mom and dad. But even now that I'm a married man with children of my own, I still want to honor and please my parents—not just because I love them, but because I want to please God.

The fear of the Lord also brings power to marriages. My wife Barb and I have been married for more than twenty years, and I love her very much. But although it's good for me to want to treat Barb right and to refrain from cheating on her simply because I don't want to hurt her, the real power to be a godly husband comes from my decision to fear the Lord and to please Him in all that I do. First and foremost, I have determined to treat my wife right and to never cheat on her because I don't want to displease my Father. Now, *that* is power!

The fear of the Lord will help you on the job as well. If you wake up every day and make the decision to please your Heavenly Father, you will do whatever God requires of you in the workplace. This is the Apostle Paul's message in Ephesians 6.

EPHESIANS 6:5-7

5 Servants, be obedient to them that are your masters according to the flesh, with fear and trembling, in singleness of your heart, as unto Christ;

6 Not with eyeservice, as menpleasers; but as the servants of Christ, doing the will of God from the heart;

7 With good will doing service, as to the Lord, and not to men.

Of course, we don't have slaves and masters today as they did when the Bible was written. But we do have employees and employers, and that means these verses apply directly to us today.

The Bible tells us that we are to be obedient to our employers "... *as unto Christ; not with eyeservice, as menpleasers* ..." (vv. 5,6). In other words, if we want to please our Heavenly Father, we will work for our employers as though we are working for Jesus Himself. And we will work hard all the time, *not* just when someone is watching us!

Ask yourself this: *If Jesus came down from Heaven and stood next to me while I was at work, what would He say about my performance? Would He be pleased at how hard I was working? Or would He be grieved because of my half-hearted approach to fulfilling my job responsibilities?*

If you fear the Lord, you won't go to work and look for ways not to do your job. You won't take long lunches or extra breaks; you won't waste time with a lot of personal phone calls; and you won't steal from your employer. If you do these things in the workplace, you are pleasing yourself instead of your Heavenly Father, and you are *not* fearing Him.

This principle is so important to your success and prosperity. You may be believing God for an increase in your finances or for a promotion at your job. But are you a faithful employee, trying to please your Heavenly Father? If so, your boss will want to promote you and give you a raise. As long as you are trying to please your Father, you will try to please your boss as well.

Fearing the Lord in Your Serving And in Your Giving

Another area in which fearing the Lord can affect your success is serving in your church. The Bible makes it clear that we're to be involved in our local church. In the Book of Acts, we see that the first Christians served each other and assisted those in leadership.

Unfortunately, many Christians never get involved in their churches. But if pleasing God was their goal, they would never be content just to attend church and not to help in some way. They would find some area of ministry in which to volunteer their time, talents, and gifts.

So in review, we see that the fear of the Lord brings God's power to your marriage and family, including the lives of your children; to your service in your local church; and to your success in your job and career.

Finally, as mentioned earlier, the fear of God brings power to your pocketbook! In fact, fearing God could be the missing ingredient to your biblical financial prosperity.

The first step on the road to financial prosperity is tithing. Sadly, pastors often have to spend a great deal of time just trying to convince their church members that they are *supposed* to tithe.

This wouldn't be the case, however, if believers walked in the fear of God and had a wholesome dread of displeasing Him. They would obey the Bible in the important area of tithing and of giving offerings into the work of God's Kingdom. As a result, the windows of Heaven would be opened in their lives and they would begin to experience for themselves what God declares in Psalm 35:27: that He *has pleasure* in the prosperity of His servants!

Let me stress one more time what this means for you personally. A flood of divine power and blessing stands ready to pour into every area of your life to bring you Heaven's abundance, success, and prosperity. And how is that flood released? By choosing to add that crucial missing ingredient to every situation of life: *walking in the fear of God*!

---

[1] W. E. Vine, Merrill F. Unger, William White, Jr., *Vine's Complete Expository Dictionary of Old and New Testament Words* (Nashville: Thomas Nelson Publishers, 1985), p. 230.

CHAPTER THREE

The Role of the Tongue

When the Word of God talks about fearing the Lord, its message is that we are to hate *all* sin as a whole. However, the Bible does seem to place a greater emphasis on one specific area of sin that we are to avoid at all costs, and it has to do with our tongue.

> PSALM 34:11–13
> 11 Come, ye children, hearken unto me: I will teach you the fear of the Lord.
> 12 What man is he that desireth life, and loveth many days, that he may see good?
> 13 Keep thy tongue from evil, and thy lips from speaking guile.

Notice that the psalmist David says he will teach us the fear of the Lord. Then he goes on to tell us the promise that is ours to claim. God will give us a long life, and we will see much good as we experience the many benefits of fearing Him.

But notice what we have to do in order to walk in the fear of God and partake of this promise. We have to *keep our tongue from evil and our lips from speaking guile.* It's interesting that of all the sins we're to hate and to avoid in life, God emphasizes one specific area: We *must* keep our mouths under control.

As we study this subject further in the Word, the connection between the fear of God and the words of our mouth will become even clearer. But for now, notice that this passage of Scripture doesn't tell us to stay away from sexual sin, stealing, cheating on our taxes, cursing, or any other sin. Of course, we know it's important to stay away from these sins as well. But in these verses, God stresses an absolutely vital key to our ultimate success in this life: *If we want to keep the fear of the Lord before our eyes, we have to control what comes out of our mouths.*

The Froward Mouth

Earlier we looked at Proverbs 8:13, where several sins that God hates are listed: *"The fear of the Lord is to hate evil: pride, and arrogancy, and the evil way, and the froward mouth, do I hate."* Notice that the last sin listed in this verse is "the froward mouth." Once again, we see that our mouths play a key role in whether or not we fear the Lord.

The Hebrew word translated "froward" implies that a froward mouth is a mouth full of fraud, one that perverts the truth or that takes truth and twists it. People with froward mouths often tell stories that have an element of truth in them, but that truth is always twisted in some way. When that happens, the truth in the story is no longer truth but rather has become a lie.

God wants us to be straightforward and honest at all times. We are not to twist the truth or to use it for our own advantage.

This is often why the Word isn't working in the lives of some Christians. They would rather tell a lie in a difficult situation than to speak the truth in love as the Bible instructs them to do (Eph. 4:15). But God is the God of truth, and He exhorts His people through the Apostle Paul, *"Lie not one to another, seeing that ye have put off the old man with his deeds; and have put on the new man, which is renewed in knowledge after the image of him that created him"* (Col. 3:9,10).

Ministers may be tempted in this area as well. That's why Paul wrote to Timothy, *"Study to shew thyself approved unto God, a workman that needeth not to be ashamed, rightly dividing the word of truth"* (2 Tim. 2:15). In the Greek language, that last phrase could also read, "taking the truth and cutting it straight."[1]

Let's look at some other scriptures that will help us understand why the mouth is such an important factor when walking in the fear of the Lord.

ROMANS 3:13-15

13 Their throat is an open sepulchre; with their tongues they have used deceit; the poison of asps is under their lips:

14 Whose mouth is full of cursing and bitterness:

15 Their feet are swift to shed blood.

PSALM 36:2,3

2 For he flattereth himself in his own eyes, until his iniquity be found to be hateful.

3 The words of his mouth are iniquity and deceit: he hath left off to be wise, and to do good.

Notice how many times "mouth," "tongue," or related words are used in these two passages. Why is God so concerned with the mouth? Because our mouths get us into trouble more than anything else does. We all have said things we shouldn't have said, even though we're saved, righteous, and created in the image of God.

Proverbs 6 contains a passage that clearly reveals how much God hates the sins of the tongue.

PROVERBS 6:16-19

16 These six things doth the Lord hate: yea, seven are an abomination unto him:

17 A proud look, a lying tongue, and hands that shed innocent blood,

18 An heart that deviseth wicked imaginations, feet that be swift in running to mischief,

19 A false witness that speaketh lies, and he that soweth discord among brethren.

Of the seven sins listed here, three of them deal directly with the tongue: 1) a lying tongue (v. 17); 2) a false witness that speaks lies (v. 19); and 3) the person who sows discord (v. 19). I believe there is actually a fourth one here regarding the tongue in verse 18, where it says, *"An heart that deviseth wicked imaginations . . . ."* When a person devises wicked imaginations (the word "deviseth" means *to fabricate things*), he is doing it in his mind. And whenever someone starts fabricating wicked imaginations in his mind, those negative thoughts will eventually come out of his mouth in the form of *words* (*see* Luke 6:45).

It cannot be emphasized enough how important it is that we fear the Lord with the things we say. If we as Christians would learn to control our tongues, we would begin to see the power of God working in and through us like never before! *In fact, the words of our mouths make the difference between success and failure in everything we do.*

The Accuser or the Advocate: Whose Side Are You On?

Recently, I heard a minister relate an analogy that really drives home just how important it is that we keep our mouths lined up with the Word of God. I want to relate that story to you; however, first allow me to address the nature of the devil's role and of Jesus' role in our lives.

33

REVELATION 12:9,10

9 And the great dragon was cast out, that old serpent, called the Devil, and Satan, which deceiveth the whole world: he was cast out into the earth, and his angels were cast out with him.

10 And I heard a loud voice saying in heaven, Now is come salvation, and strength, and the kingdom of our God, and the power of his Christ: for the accuser of our brethren [the devil] is cast down, which accused them before our God day and night.

From these verses, we know that the devil was cast out of Heaven. When he left Heaven, he came down here to earth. Second Corinthians 4:4 says he is now the god of this age and the god of the world we live in.

So what is the devil doing down here on this earth? Revelation 12:10 tells us that part of his job is *to accuse people*. In the Greek language, the phrase "the accuser of our brethren" means *the one who brings accusations against someone*. The devil is an accuser, and his role is to bring accusations against Christians.

Now let's take a look at one of Jesus' roles in our lives today. First John 2:1 reads, *"My little children, these things write I unto you, that ye sin not. And if any man sin, we have an advocate with the Father, Jesus Christ the righteous."* We see from this verse that Jesus acts as our Advocate before the Father when we sin.

The word "advocate" is the Greek word *parakletos*. It's the same word that is used for "Comforter" in John 14:16 and John 16:7. According to *The Amplified Bible*, it also means *Counselor, Helper, Advocate, Intercessor, Strengthener,* and *Standby.*[2] In addition, *parakletos* refers to *someone who pleads favorably the case of another.*[3] In other words, when Jesus is pleading our case, He is pleading it favorably for us. Jesus is on our side!

Now I'll endeavor to relate the minister's analogy that aptly illustrates the roles of Satan, the accuser, and of Jesus, our Advocate. First, picture a courtroom. In the center of that courtroom, God sits as Judge. Seated in front of God the Judge is the prosecution and the defense. The prosecutor is the devil. He's the one who has brought the accusations forward. On the other side is the defense, who is Jesus, our Advocate.

It's important to note that the accuser and the Advocate never switch sides. Jesus never walks over to the prosecution and offers to help the devil and his team. And the devil never offers assistance to the defense!

So we have a courtroom with a Judge, a prosecutor, and a Defense Attorney. And who is the one on trial? The Christian who has sinned.

When we do something wrong, the devil immediately begins to accuse us, and he loves to keep reminding us of what we have done. We've all felt the condemnation that the devil throws at us by attacking our minds and telling us over and over what unworthy failures we are.

But the devil doesn't stop there. He seeks to cause even greater destruction by making sure other Christian brothers and sisters find out what we have done. Too often these fellow Christians then surround us with their words of condemnation and judgment. And before we know it, those Christians have told others about our sin, and the cycle continues to grow and to perpetuate itself.

Has that ever happened to you? Have you ever made a mistake that someone found out about and started telling to others? Sadly, I think some in the Body of Christ believe that this is their ministry. Soon it isn't just the devil who is accusing you; it's your Christian family as well!

It is up to us to make sure that we never make this mistake of siding with the accuser. We need to realize that the moment we start accusing a brother or sister, we have begun to help the prosecutor, the devil himself, build his case against him or her. We're actually working for the enemy! We've joined his team!

At the point when Christians begin to accuse a brother or sister of doing wrong, the devil can usually just step back and let them take over. (Unfortunately, too often Christians are the ones who do the devil's dirty work of accusation, *not* unbelievers.)

Eventually some may begin to feel guilty about accusing their brother. Suddenly they feel the burden to help their brother and to lift him up in prayer, so they get a group together to pray for him.

Isn't it interesting how that works? First, these Christians joined the devil's team and became accusers by talking against their fellow believer. Then all of a sudden they want to switch to the Advocate's side in order to offer up a prayer!

But Jesus is different. Even if the accused person has done wrong—even if he is guilty as charged—the Advocate will never accuse him of it. Jesus will never go over to the accuser's side and begin to incriminate a Christian. His role is always the Advocate, *never* the accuser.

What does that mean for the Christians who joined the prosecution team at the trial of their fellow believer? Before their prayers can be effective, they will need to repent of using their tongues to help the accuser present his case.

Some might think they're justified in talking about certain situations in another Christian's life because they know the accusations are true. But even if the information is correct, it is still wrong for them to stand in judgment against that person if they are going to follow the example of their Advocate, Jesus.

In the courtroom, the accuser of the brethren says, "This person committed a sin."

Jesus the Advocate responds, "That sin has been washed in My blood."

The accuser of the brethren then says, "Here are fifteen Christians who all agree that he's guilty. I have a solid case against him."

Jesus responds again: "I don't see what you see. This person is clean because I see him washed in the blood that I shed. I'm the Advocate, and I'm standing up for him to defend him before the righteous Judge."

Grieving the Holy Spirit

The scene I've just described isn't entirely made up. It is an analogy using a courtroom scenario to depict a spiritual truth. From Heaven's perspective, this is what actually goes on in the spiritual realm.

Unfortunately, in most cases, all the devil has to do is make sure that one or two Christians hear about the sin of another believer; then he can step back and let them take over. Most often they will verbally beat up their brother or sister and do everything they can to destroy him or her.

That's why Ephesians 4:29 commands us, *"Let no corrupt* [the Greek says "rotten"] *communication proceed out of your mouth, but that which is good to the use of edifying, that it may minister grace unto the hearers."* That word "grace" implies something *uplifting* and *edifying*. We shouldn't speak anything that doesn't uplift and edify others.

Verse 30 goes on to say, *"And grieve not the holy Spirit of God, whereby ye are sealed unto the day of redemption."* How do we grieve the Holy Ghost? By siding in with the accuser and allowing corrupt or rotten words to come out of our mouths.

Here's another way to look at this: The Bible says we are all part of the Body of Christ. Therefore, when we talk about another Christian, in reality we are talking about Christ. We would never think of gossiping about Jesus, but that's exactly what we are doing when we gossip about a fellow brother or sister!

Once we make a firm decision to walk in the fear of the Lord, we must then continually strive to remain on the Advocate's side. In the past, we may have sided with the accuser one moment and then run over to God's side the next moment to "stand in faith" because we needed something from Him. But it's time to realize that it just doesn't work that way in the Kingdom of God.

We can't say to our spouse, "Honey, did you hear about what So-and-so did?" and then expect to lay hands on our sick child the next moment and effectively believe God for his healing. James 1:6–8 provides a reality check for us along this line.

> JAMES 1:6–8
> 6 But let him ask in faith, nothing wavering. For he that wavereth is like a wave of the sea driven with the wind and tossed.
> 7 For let not that man think that he shall receive any thing of the Lord.

8 A double minded man is unstable in all his ways.

We cannot be double-minded in our choice to walk in the fear of God. If we are to enjoy His many blessings and achieve the success He has ordained for our lives, we must remain constant in our determination to keep a watch on our mouths and speak only in line with our Advocate in Heaven!

---

[1] James Strong, "Greek Dictionary of the New Testament," *Strong's Exhaustive Concordance* (Tulsa: American Christian College Press), p. 52, # 3718.

[2] *The Amplified Bible* (Zondervan Corporation and Lockman Foundation, 1987), p. 1237.

[3] Greek Dictionary of the New Testament, p. 55, #3875.

CHAPTER FOUR

The Judgment Seat of Christ

M ost adults probably remember that when they were young, their parents encouraged or discouraged certain behavior in them by attaching certain rewards or consequences to their actions. In fact, if you're a parent, you probably do that with your own children as well. More than likely, you tell them that they'll be rewarded for good behavior and punished for bad behavior. The rewards may include an allowance, a privilege, or your permission to do something they want to do. The punishment may be a spanking or a privilege taken from them.

When parents follow this method of training, they are basically telling their children, "I will bless you by giving you a reward if you do what's right. But if you do something wrong, there will be negative consequences for your actions."

God uses similar methods to get us motivated to fear Him. (Remember, to fear God doesn't mean to be afraid of Him, but to have a wholesome dread of ever displeasing Him.) His Word teaches us that if we live the way He wants us to live, we will experience His rewards.

On the other hand, if we live in disobedience to God's Word, we will suffer negative consequences for our actions. Ultimately, we won't be able to experience all that God intended for us on this earth. We won't enjoy the peace, joy, and prosperity He wants us to have.

It's important to keep in mind, however, that such consequences never occur because God is withholding His blessings. Rather, we stop His blessings from getting through to us through our disobedience.

A Fundamental Doctrine For All Christians

There is another consequence that believers will face one day for their actions here on this earth—the Judgment Seat of Christ.

2 CORINTHIANS 5:9,10

9 Wherefore we labour, that, whether present or absent, we may be accepted of him.

10 For we must all appear before the judgment seat of Christ; that every one may receive the things

done in his body, according to that he hath done, whether it be good or bad.

This isn't a very popular topic in the Church today, but it is something that all Christians, without exception, will face.

The good news is that if you're standing before the Judgment Seat one day, it means you have received Christ as your Savior and you are going to spend eternity in Heaven. However, there is more to eternal life than just getting to Heaven.

The term "judgment seat" in the Greek refers to a place where a judge sits and hands out either consequences or rewards. Christians, then, will either be rewarded or punished for their works when they stand before the Judgment Seat of Christ. Their only release from judgment is repentance.

Notice that verse 10 says, ". . . *we must all appear before the judgment seat of Christ . . . .*" This is not an option. It isn't a biblical doctrine that you can choose whether or not you want to believe. You can choose, for example, not to believe in healing—and you probably won't get healed. But you *will* appear before the Judgment Seat of Christ whether you believe it or not!

Some Christians may think they'll somehow escape judgment for the wrong actions for which they never repented. Perhaps they are such smooth talkers here on earth that they are able to get themselves out of any situation. But there won't be any smooth talking on that day. Jesus will look right through every believer with those eyes of fire, and he or she will just melt in His Presence.

It's sad that many Christians have never heard teaching on this subject. This is especially true because the Judgment Seat is the last of the six basic doctrines listed in the Book of Hebrews that all Christians are supposed to understand.

HEBREWS 6:1,2

1 Therefore leaving the principles of the doctrine of Christ, let us go on unto perfection; not laying again the foundation of repentance from dead works, and of faith toward God,

2 Of the doctrine of baptisms, and of laying on of hands, and of resurrection of the dead, and of eternal judgment.

The Judgment Seat is a fundamental doctrine that should be established in our lives. We should get saved, get grounded in teaching about these six basic doctrines, and then move on from there as we ". . . *go on unto perfection . . .*" (v. 1).

What Are Your Motives?

It's important to understand how the Kingdom of God works. For one thing, we shouldn't confuse the judgment of our deeds as Christians with the Great White Throne Judgment. We will go to Heaven because we accepted the blood of Jesus that was shed for us. That has nothing to do with our own works.

If you've accepted the redemption Jesus purchased for you at Calvary, you are saved. And if you're saved, you are a child and an heir of God. According to Romans 8, you will receive an inheritance. In fact, the Bible says the Holy Ghost is a down payment toward your inheritance (Eph. 1:14).

But there is another side to this. In addition to our inheritance, we will receive rewards based on how we live on earth. People who have done works out of the right motives of love and a desire to please God will receive greater rewards than those who did right things for wrong reasons. That should be a powerful motivator for us to guard our hearts and to live right!

It's interesting to consider how this may work. It's very possible that one Christian may be rewarded for doing something while another Christian is *not* rewarded for doing exactly the same thing. Why? Because one had pure motives, and the other one didn't.

That's why it's so important that we don't judge people. We have no idea what their motives are. Only God can judge the motives of a person's heart.

Romans 14:4 confirms this message: *"Who art thou that judgest another man's servant? to his own master he standeth or falleth. Yea, he shall be holden up: for God is able to make him stand."* The Apostle Paul tells us in this verse that we have no right to judge another person. We will all answer to God regarding our motives and the attitudes of our hearts.

Paul goes on to talk about the day we stand before the Judgment Seat of Christ.

> ROMANS 14:10–12
> 10 But why dost thou judge thy brother? or why dost thou set at nought thy brother? for we shall all stand before the judgment seat of Christ.
> 11 For it is written, As I live, saith the Lord, every knee shall bow to me, and every tongue shall confess to God.
> 12 So then every one of us shall give account of himself to God.

Again, we see from this passage that we can't judge our brothers or sisters in the Lord, because each one of us will stand before God on that Day and give an account of our lives.

Paul also talks about this Day in First Corinthians 4:5: *"Therefore judge nothing before the time, until the Lord come, who both will bring to light the hidden [secret] things of darkness, and will make manifest the counsels of the hearts: and then shall every man have praise of God."* The meaning of the word "counsels" in the Greek is *purposes.* This passage therefore teaches us that God will one day manifest, or reveal, the purposes of our hearts. On that day, we will be judged according to the motives behind our deeds on this earth.

Let the Judgment Seat Change the Way You Live Today!

Second Corinthians 5:11 says, *"Knowing therefore the terror of the Lord, we persuade men . . . ."* The word "knowing" in this passage is the key. You have to know or have a revelation of something before it can effectively motivate you to live differently. The only way for the Judgment Seat to become known to you is to meditate on scriptures about the reality of that topic until they become rooted in your spirit.

The word "terror" in Second Corinthians 5:11 is the same Greek word that is used for *fear*. So we could say, "Knowing therefore the fear of the Lord, we persuade men." Why did Paul persuade men? He knew about, or had a revelation of, the fear of the Lord. In the same way, if we want to please our Father, we will also tell others about His love and the salvation that Jesus purchased for them on the Cross.

Too many Christians today have the attitude that they can live any way they want and then simply ask God to forgive them. Then once they're forgiven, they think they can go right back to the same sinful lifestyle and just keep asking for forgiveness again and again. They don't understand that true repentance means a 180-degree turnaround, that there is to be no return to the sin for which they have repented.

When you understand the fear of the Lord, you won't continue to commit the same sins over and over again. Instead you'll think to yourself, *I fear God, and I don't want to displease Him. And one day I'm going to stand before the Judgment Seat of Christ for this, so I'd better make a change!*

Don't Be 'Hardly Saved'

First Peter 4:18 reads, *"And if the righteous scarcely be saved, where shall the ungodly and the sinner appear?"* In the Greek, "scarcely" means *hardly* or *barely.* This verse reveals that it is possible for a Christian to be hardly saved. People who fit in this category may even go to church once or twice a week, but they don't allow the Word to dictate or influence how they conduct their lives. They are "hardly" or "barely" saved. In other words, even though it's great that they go to church, God has so much more for them.

In Revelation 3:16, Jesus refers to these people as "lukewarm" Christians: *"So then because thou art lukewarm, and neither cold nor hot, I will spue thee out of my mouth."* In the Greek, the last part of that verse reads, "I'll *vomit* you out of My mouth."

Jesus wants us to be either hot or cold because there is too much compromise and hypocrisy involved with lukewarm Christianity. Only at those extremes of hot or cold are we displaying a clear picture of right and wrong.

If we are lukewarm, we will have very little godly effect on those around us.

What is the "cure" for ineffective, barely saved, lukewarm Christianity? The knowledge that someday God will require an answer from you regarding how you have lived on this earth. So instead of being satisfied with being "barely" saved, determine to sell out completely to God. Then you'll look forward to the day when you see Jesus face-to-face and hear those words you have longed to hear from Him: "Well done, My good and faithful servant"!

CHAPTER FIVE

The Rewards of Fearing the Lord

I n the last chapter, we saw that one way God motivates us to fear Him is by making sure we have knowledge of the consequences associated with our actions. That's the discipline side of motivation. But we also saw that there is another side of divine motivation—the rewards side. Many scriptures teach us that God will reward us when we fear Him.

For some people, the discipline side is enough to motivate them. For others, however, focusing only on the consequences will not work. In fact, it may drive them further from God. They need to know the rewards that are offered to those who fear the Lord and walk in His ways.

Long Life

The first reward can be found in Proverbs 10:27, which says, *"The fear of the Lord prolongeth days: but the years of the wicked shall be shortened."* The word "prolongeth" means *adds to.*[1] If we fear God, He will add days to our lives.

God's original plan was for man to physically live forever. Physical death was introduced only after Adam and Eve disobeyed God and allowed sin to enter their lives. According to Genesis 5:5, Adam lived to be 930 years old. But as we continue to read the Bible and move further away from Adam, we see that people began to live shorter and shorter lives.

Sin is the force that cuts our lives short. But if we walk in the fear of the Lord, which includes staying away from sin, we will live long. Although we'll never live as long as Adam did, God specifically promises us long life if we will fear Him and keep His commandments.

A Satisfied Life

As we have seen, the first reward for fearing the Lord is *prolonged days* or *a long life.* The second reward is *a satisfied life.*

Long life is a wonderful thing, but not if life is miserable! If you talk to some people, even Christians, they'll tell you that they'd rather die than to continue living with the problems they are facing right now. For example, a person who is having serious marriage or health problems might be tempted to believe that death would be a welcome relief. But that is never true for the individual who fears the Lord.

Proverbs 19:23 says, *"The fear of the Lord tendeth to life: and he that hath it shall abide satisfied; he shall not be visited with evil."* The phrase "tendeth to life" is again referring to the first promise of living a long life. But the second part of the verse tells us something else: Not only will we live long, but we'll live *satisfied* and *without evil*!

What does being satisfied mean? It means you're happy with your job, happy with your marriage, happy with your kids, happy with your health, happy with your financial situation. You're happy because God has satisfied you like only He can!

A vital key to being satisfied with our lives is to be in the center of God's will. God has a specific plan for each of us that will bring us satisfaction and success in our lives—but His plan is revealed to us only as we fear Him.

Healing

The third reward for fearing the Lord can be found in Malachi 4:2: *"But unto you that fear my name shall the Sun of righteousness arise with healing in his wings . . . ."*

If you fear God, then the "Sun of righteousness," who is Jesus, will manifest His *healing power* to you.

How does this third promise of healing tie into the first two rewards for fearing the Lord? God wants us to live long, satisfied lives. But can we ever truly be satisfied if we spend our lives living in pain or battling sickness or disease? Just as sickness and disease are not blessings, neither is a life filled with doctors' offices, surgeries, and medications. Physical pain and sickness not only slow us down and hinder us from doing the things God wants us to do, they also rob us of our financial blessings.

Through Jesus, God made provision for us to receive healing. It is His will for us to walk in divine health every day of our lives so we can do His work and be satisfied during the time He's given us on the earth.

A Safe Refuge

So far, we've seen that God wants us to live long, satisfied, healthy lives. The fourth reward for fearing the Lord can be found in Proverbs 14:26: *"In the fear of the Lord is strong confidence: and his children shall have a place of refuge."*

If you fear the Lord, He will be a refuge for you. He will be a strong tower you can run to (Ps. 61:3; Prov. 18:10). He will be your Protector. And when you face overwhelming trials and circumstances, fearing the Lord will give you strong confidence in Him and in His ability to deliver you.

Freedom From Sin

Proverbs 14:27 continues, *"The fear of the Lord is a fountain of life, to depart from the snares of death."* In the Hebrew, this verse literally means, "The fear of the Lord is a source of life so that you might depart or turn from the noose or the hook of death." This is the fifth promise: *The fear of God gives you the ability to turn from sin and be free of its hook that once had you snared.*

Sin has a hook that gets in a person and won't let go. That's why people tend to struggle to overcome such things as alcohol, drugs, cigarettes, and pornography. Sometimes these sins are merely labeled as addictions, as part of a person's makeup. But the Bible declares that there is a spiritual side to all these sinful strongholds.

Too often people, including Christians, don't recognize the spiritual aspect of their addictions and thus try to overcome them only by natural means. As a result of this error, many Christians have no victory over sin and don't look or act differently than the world.

But the God-fearing Christian is set free from the hook of sin because he partakes of the Source of life on a moment-by-moment basis. And as a result, he is an overcoming, victorious Christian!

Prosperity

The sixth reward for fearing the Lord is *biblical financial prosperity*. Proverbs 22:4 says, *"By humility and the fear of the Lord are riches, and honour, and life."* The word "riches" in this verse is the Hebrew word for *wealth*, and the word "honour" is the Hebrew word for *glory*. Thus, this verse tells us that when we fear God, we will grow in wealth and experience His glory in our lives.

Biblical prosperity is God's will for His children. But notice that according to Proverbs 22:4, wealth, glory, and abundant life result from "humility and the fear of the Lord."

You might say, "But I thought prosperity came through tithing and giving offerings. Do you mean that if I just fear God, I'll be wealthy?"

That's exactly what I mean. To fear God means that you'd never do anything to displease Him and that you obey the Word of God. Thus, if you fear God, you will tithe and give offerings! All these scriptural truths are tied in together. Tithing and giving offerings are vital to your prosperity, but so are your attitudes and motives.

God will never bless us financially until we walk in humility before Him. Otherwise, we'd take the credit for our prosperity. Therefore, the scriptural way to receive financial increase is by giving tithes and offerings as we humble ourselves before the Lord and fear Him in all that we do.

True biblical prosperity—the kind that has no sorrow with it (Prov. 10:22)—can only come when we abide by the guidelines in the Word. James 4:2 and 3 confronts this issue: *"Ye lust, and have not: ye kill, and desire to have, and cannot obtain: ye fight and war, yet ye have not, because ye ask not. Ye ask, and receive not, because ye ask amiss, that ye may consume it upon your lusts."*

The word "amiss" means *with wrong attitudes and motives.* What is an example of a wrong motive when asking God for something? The next part of the verse tells us: to desire things only for the purpose of consuming them for ourselves.

God doesn't want us to be selfish. Yes, He wants to bless us, and He wants us to prosper. But our ultimate goal for prosperity should always be to give into God's Kingdom and to help others.

This is how humility ties into prosperity. When you humble yourself before God, you set your own wants and desires aside and submit yourself to *His* desires and *His* will.

James 4:6 goes on to say, *". . . Wherefore he saith, God resisteth the proud, but giveth grace unto the humble."* The word "resisteth" means *to oppose* or *to array against in battle.* With that definition in mind, we can say, "God opposes or arrays Himself in battle against the proud, but He gives grace to the humble."

Keep in mind that this verse was written to Christians—to those who are born again—*not* to unbelievers. So even if you're a believer, when you have pride in your life, you are on the opposite side of God!

It's also important to understand that biblical humility deals with your relationship with God rather than your relationship with others. James 4:7 makes this point: *"Submit yourselves therefore to God. Resist the devil, and he will flee from you."* In the Greek language, the word for "submit" means *to arrange yourself under.*

Many times Christians read only the last part of that verse—and when they try to resist the devil, they fail. These Christians never seem to be able to get the victory over sin, sickness, and poverty. But there is a reason they're not living as overcomers: They haven't submitted to, or arranged themselves under, God and His Word!

James 4:10 again drives home this point: *"Humble yourselves in the sight of the Lord, and he shall lift you up."* In other words, fear the Lord by arranging yourself under His authority, and *then* you will have the power to overcome!

Mercy

Psalm 103:13 says, *"Like as a father pitieth his children, so the Lord pitieth them that fear him."* The

word "pitieth" means *to have compassion or mercy on.*
Thus, the seventh promise or reward for fearing the Lord
is that He will show compassion and mercy toward us.
In fact, verse 17 says that throughout eternity, He will
never cease to show His mercy toward us as we choose
to walk in the fear of the Lord: *"But the mercy of the
Lord is from everlasting to everlasting upon them that
fear him . . . ."*

What is mercy? Mercy is the treatment we experience when we receive something good we don't deserve.
Forgiveness is a good example of this. Even though we
don't deserve it, God will always forgive us when we
confess our sin to Him (1 John 1:9). It should be clear to
us all that we couldn't do without this particular reward!

Revelation

The eighth and final promise that we'll study can be
found in Psalm 25:14: *"The secret of the Lord is with
them that fear him; and he will shew them his
covenant."*

This verse promises that as you walk in the fear of
God, you will receive *revelation* from Him. In fact, this
scripture actually provides "two promises in one." The
first is that *God will show you secrets.* The second is that
He will show you His covenant.

How will these revelations help you? First, God
gives you revelations to help you experience victory in
your own life. Whenever you receive a revelation

regarding a truth in God's Word (in other words, whenever He shows you another facet of His covenant), you
become better equipped to walk in that particular truth.
Each revelation God gives you produces greater victory
in some area of your life.

Second, God gives you revelations to enable you to
more effectively minister to others. For example, in
order to help you be a better parent, God may reveal to
you a trial that is taking place in your child's life. Not
only will that revelation help you pray about the matter
more effectively, but you'll also be more equipped to
discern God's guidance in handling the situation.

Let's review the rewards of fearing the Lord one
more time. When we determine to walk in the fear of
God in every area of our lives, we put ourselves in position to enjoy the benefits of:

A long life

A satisfied life

Divine healing

A safe refuge

Freedom from sin

Prosperity

Mercy

Divine revelation

It's enough to make you wonder why we would
ever choose to live one day doing things our own way

for our own selfish reasons, doesn't it? After all, the fullness of God's abundant life is waiting on the other side of our decision to fear the Lord!

---

[1] Strong, "Hebrew and Chaldee Dictionary of the Old Testament," p. 50, #3254.

CHAPTER SIX

The 'Dirty Word' in the New Testament

B efore we were saved, many of us used ungodly or dirty language. Thank God, we've been delivered from that! But Christianity has its own "dirty words." These aren't dirty because they're vulgar or profane. I just call them "dirty words" because people don't like to hear them. One of these words is *holiness*.

Many people don't like to hear about holiness, even though the subject is found throughout the Word. Most of the time holiness is taught as a list of do's and don'ts. But although there are certainly things one should or should not do in order to live a holy life, holiness actually means *being separate from the world.*

Perfecting Holiness

Second Corinthians 7:1 shows us the connection between holiness and the fear of God: *"Having therefore these promises, dearly beloved, let us cleanse ourselves from all filthiness of the flesh and spirit, perfecting holiness in the fear of God."*

Notice first that the fear of God helps you perfect holiness. You can't perfect holiness without walking in the fear of the Lord, for the two are integrally linked together. When you hate what God hates and you have a wholesome dread of ever displeasing Him, you will separate yourself from the sinful lifestyle of the world. That choice will then cause you to live a more holy life.

The word "perfecting" means *to come to a complete end*—in other words, *to finish*. But the definition in the Greek also indicates that it is an ongoing process; it is *not* something that happens overnight.

If you've been saved and walking in the Word for several years, you can probably look back and see that you're walking in more holiness now than you were three, five, or ten years ago. At the same time, you probably can't see a difference in how holy you are today compared to two or three days ago. Why is this? *Because holiness is a process.*

Growing in holiness is like physical growth. If you're a parent, for example, you don't notice how much your children are growing on a day-to-day basis.

64

But when you visit with relatives or friends who haven't seen your family for a while, one of the first things they'll do is comment about how much your children are growing up.

It's important to keep in mind that holiness is different for every person because God deals with people in different ways concerning sin in their lives. I've learned over the years as a pastor that I can't tell people what they're allowed to do and what they're not allowed to do. My responsibility is simply to show people what the Word of God says, and God will handle it from there. He'll work with them and prune what He wants to prune from their lives so they can grow in holiness before Him.

Motivations for Perfecting Holiness

Look again at Second Corinthians 7:1. Paul starts out by saying, *"Having therefore these promises . . . ."* This tells us that our motivation for perfecting holiness should be the fact that we possess the promises Paul had just discussed. Let's look at the verses that come right before this verse to find out what promises he was talking about.

> 2 CORINTHIANS 6:16
> 16 And what agreement hath the temple of God with idols? for ye are the temple of the living God; as God hath said, I will dwell in them, and walk in them; and I will be their God, and they shall be my people.

God's first promise is that *He will dwell in us.* That's why holiness is an issue for us as Christians. If we are born again, we are the temple of God. God Himself is actually dwelling in us in the Person of the Holy Spirit. Because of this, we should desire to keep ourselves pure.

God's second promise is found in the same verse: *". . . I will be their God, and they shall be my people."* This second promise motivates us to perfect holiness in our lives because *God is our God and we are His people,* and we should therefore desire to do what pleases Him.

2 CORINTHIANS 6:17
17 Wherefore come out from among them, and be ye separate, saith the Lord, and touch not the unclean thing; and I will receive you.

The third promise that motivates us to perfect holiness is that *God receives us.* This phrase "I will receive you" actually means "I will entreat favor upon you." Thus, if we separate ourselves from the world and perfect holiness in God's sight, He will give us His favor.

What does it mean to enjoy the favor of God? It means that everything you do is blessed. You are blessed going in and blessed going out (Deut. 28:6). You are the head and not the tail, above and not beneath (Deut. 28:13). In other words, God's favor gives you victory in every area of life!

2 CORINTHIANS 6:18

18 And will be a Father unto you, and ye shall be
my sons and daughters, saith the Lord Almighty.

God's fourth promise that motivates us to perfect
holiness is that He will be our very own Father—and as a
loving Father, He will protect and take care of us.

Parents are very protective of their children. In fact,
most parents will do whatever is necessary to protect
their children from harm. So is God any different?
Absolutely not! If we fear Him and separate ourselves
from the world's way of doing things, He will make sure
that no harm comes to us.

We've seen from these verses in Second Corinthians
6 that God made four promises to us:

1. He will dwell in us.

2. He will be our God.

3. He will give us His favor.

4. He will be a Father to us.

Now, let's go back to Second Corinthians 7:1:
*"Having therefore these promises . . . let us cleanse our-
selves from all filthiness of the flesh and spirit, perfecting holiness in the fear of God."* This verse is saying that
the four promises God made to us in Second Corinthians
6:16–18 should motivate us to perfect holiness in our
lives. We should want to please God and allow Him to
prune from our lives whatever doesn't belong.

One more thing on this subject of pruning: When we think of God pruning things from our lives, we often think of Him cutting off the "big sins," such as adultery, fornication, lying, or stealing. But sometimes the "twig" to be pruned may be something that, although not sin in and of itself, has become sin for us simply because it's getting in the way of our walk with God.

For example, one of the things God personally spoke to me about in times past was becoming a better listener, especially in regard to my wife and children. This "pruning" issue wasn't a sin I had to overcome; rather, it was an area of improvement I needed to make in my life.

Getting Down to the Nitty-Gritty

Any teaching on holiness cannot deny what the Bible clearly states: There are certain actions and behaviors that shouldn't be a part of any Christian's life. In today's politically correct culture, people get offended when these scriptures are mentioned. But God isn't concerned with our being politically correct; He still expects us to follow every part of His Word.

Let's look at one such "politically incorrect" passage of Scripture.

1 CORINTHIANS 6:9,10
9 Know ye not that the unrighteous shall not
inherit the kingdom of God? Be not deceived: neither fornicators, nor idolaters, nor adulterers, nor

> effeminate, nor abusers of themselves with
> mankind,
> 10 Nor thieves, nor covetous, nor drunkards, nor
> revilers, nor extortioners, shall inherit the kingdom
> of God.

Here God gives us a list of people who will not go to Heaven. It is important for us to understand how He defines these sins so we can make sure we never fall into that list!

First, a *fornicator* is simply an unmarried person who is getting involved in forbidden sexual situations. An *adulterer*, on the other hand, is someone who is married but is having sexual relations with someone other than his or her spouse.

The next people listed are *idolaters*. Now, in our society we don't have golden images or manmade idols to which we physically bow down and worship, so we may think we're clear of that designation. But an idol is actually anything in our lives that we put before God.

Television is probably the most popular idol in today's society. Many people don't go to church or spend time with God because they're too busy watching television or because they don't want to miss their favorite program.

The next two, the *effeminate* and the *abusers of themselves with mankind*, are closely related. The meaning of "effeminate" in the Greek is actually *homosexual*, and "abusers of themselves with mankind" refers to *people who participate in sodomite acts*.

It's definitely not popular in our society to say that homosexuality is a sin, but that's what the Bible says. Does that mean God hates homosexuals? Absolutely not! Jesus died on the Cross for them because He loves them just as much as anyone else—and we Christians should love them too!

Unfortunately, portions of the Church have bought into the world's view on this subject. There are now some ministers who publicly declare that they're homosexuals and that they can't change because "God made them that way." But just because someone has a desire to do something doesn't mean that is what God wants him to do. For example, some people desire to rob banks, but we'd never say, "Well, that's just the way God made those people, and He wants them to act on their desire to rob a bank!"

How horrible God would be if He created some people to behave a certain way and then told them they couldn't go to Heaven because of that same behavior! Homosexuality is a sin, but Christians have the power through the Holy Spirit to overcome it, just as they have the power to overcome any other sin.

Next on the list of those who will not enter Heaven are *thieves*. Everyone seems to know the definition of a thief. However, most Christians believe that as long as they haven't held up a store or stolen a car, they don't have to worry about fitting into this category. They fail to recognize that there are other ways of stealing. For example, many Christians rob their employers every day when they go to work and don't do what they're supposed to do!

The next group, the *covetous*, are also barred from entering Heaven according to First Corinthians 6:10. To be "covetous" means *to possess an eager desire to gain increase in one's life, but through wrong or sinful methods.*

Sadly, some ministers are guilty of this when they try to coerce or force people to give offerings. That's why the Bible says, *"Every man according as he purposeth in his heart, so let him give; not grudgingly . . . ."* (2 Cor. 9:7). We're supposed to give as we believe God wants us to give, not because we feel pressured by any person.

The next category listed in First Corinthians 6:10 is the *drunkard*, which refers to *someone who is intoxicated.* We usually think of intoxication as being drunk on alcohol or high on drugs. But this word actually refers to putting any chemical in our bodies to distort how we feel or act.

As Christians, we shouldn't rely on any manmade substance to change the way we feel or act. That's why God gave us the Holy Spirit. His role is to dwell in us and change us from the inside out.

The last two types of people mentioned in First Corinthians 6:10 are the *revilers* and *extortioners*. Revilers are those who are always looking for mischief, and extortioners are people who always take advantage of others.

After listing these sinful lifestyles in the previous verses, verse 11 begins by saying, *"And such were some of you . . . ."* In other words, once we're saved, the sins listed in verses 9 and 10 should describe the way we *were*, not the way we *are.*

That same verse continues, *". . . But ye are washed, but ye are sanctified, but ye are justified in the name of the Lord Jesus, and by the Spirit of our God."* How did we become free from sin in our lives? When we became born again, the blood of Jesus washed away our sins, and the Holy Ghost gave us the power to overcome every sinful stronghold. We should *never* go back to the sinful things we used to do!

God Wants to Protect His Property

You may look at these verses in First Corinthians 6 as well as other scripture references and think to yourself, *See, it's all about a bunch of dos and don'ts.* You can look at it that way if you want to, or you can understand that God is your Father and He cares for you. He knows what is best for your life. He knows what will harm you and what will lead you astray. You can either listen to what God says and open the way for Him to bless you, or you can choose to do your own thing and struggle through life.

First Corinthians 6:19 says, *"What? know ye not that your body is the temple of the Holy Ghost which is in you, which ye have of God, and ye are not your own?"* According to this verse, if we have given our lives to Christ, our bodies have become temples of the Holy Spirit and are no longer our own. In other words, we have no right to do anything we want, because our bodies are God's property. On the other hand, He has every right to provide us with rules and guidelines to live by in order to protect His property.

Finally, verse 20 goes on to say, *"For ye are bought with a price: therefore glorify God in your body, and in your spirit, which are God's."* The bottom line is this: The reason we should become holy is to glorify God in our bodies.

The Chastening of the Lord

We know God wants us to be holy, but what does He do to get us to that place in our walk with Him?

The awesome part about our Heavenly Father is that He doesn't just tell us to do something and then leave us on our own. He always makes sure we have what we need to obey Him. This role of the Father is talked about in Hebrews 12.

HEBREWS 12:9,10

9 Furthermore we have had fathers of our flesh [natural fathers] which corrected us, and we gave them reverence [we honored them]: shall we not

THE MISSING INGREDIENT TO SUCCESS

> much rather be in subjection unto [come under the
> authority of] the Father of spirits, and live?
> 10 For they verily for a few days chastened us after
> their own pleasure; but he [God] for our profit, that
> we might be partakers of his holiness.

In other words, our natural fathers disciplined or
chastened us so we would act the way they wanted us to
act. Our fathers did it "after their own pleasure" or as
they thought best. But notice what verse 10 says: God
chastens us not for His own pleasure, but *for our profit*
or *for our own benefit*. And what is the reason He does
this? "*. . . That we might be partakers of his holiness*"
(v. 10). God corrects or disciplines us in order to help us
become more holy.

So exactly what *is* the Lord's chastening? Some
religious people have told us that God's chastening
comes in the form of sickness, disease, and personal
tragedy. According to this erroneous thinking, if you are
driving home from work one day and you lose control
of your car, hit a telephone pole, and land in the hospi-
tal with serious injuries, it could all be the result of your
loving Father's need to discipline you! Or perhaps God
will give you cancer one day in order to teach you
something. This is what people have told us, but that is
a warped view of God.

What would we say if we heard that a natural
father had made his children sick to discipline them?
And what if that father sat down next to his children

while they were lying in bed sick with a fever and in pain and told them that he had a few things he needed to teach them? Would we perceive him as a loving and kind father?

Absolutely not! We would say that man was evil and needed to be punished for harming his children. Yet this is exactly the kind of behavior that many people attribute to God!

When bad things happen to people, some Christians will say, "Well, God must be teaching them a lesson. He must have needed to get through to them."

But that isn't how God works at all. If it was, we would be foolish to want to serve Him. But we serve a loving God who is a Father to us!

Then how *does* God chasten us? Second Timothy 3:16 tells us: *"All scripture is given by inspiration of God, and is profitable for doctrine, for reproof, for correction, for instruction in righteousness."*

In the Greek, one meaning of the word translated "instruction" is *chastening*. Thus, the way God chastens you is with His Word. Often as you hear the Word being preached, the Holy Spirit will convict your heart about areas in your life that are not in line with the Word. When this happens, God is chastening you by gently and lovingly showing you where you're falling short.

Hebrews 12:11 goes on to say, *"Now no chastening for the present seemeth to be joyous, but grievous . . . ."*

Just as the discipline we receive from our natural fathers makes us uncomfortable, so also does God's discipline in our lives. In other words, it doesn't feel good when God points out to us the areas of our lives we need to work on, because that means we have to change.

Yet just as natural discipline helps us become better people later on in life, Hebrews 12:11 says something similar about God's discipline: *". . . Afterward it yieldeth the peaceable fruit of righteousness unto them which are exercised thereby."* If we will obey God, we will reap the fruit of our obedience in a harvest of divine peace, righteousness, and abundant blessing.

In John 15:2, Jesus says, *". . . Every branch that beareth fruit, he purgeth it, that it may bring forth more fruit."* The word "purgeth" relates to *pruning*.

If you've ever trimmed a tree, you know that dead branches always get cut off. Well, when we get saved, we still carry a lot of the sins and attitudes of the world. Those are all dead branches that God wants to trim off in order to make us stronger so we can bear more fruit. He does that through the preaching of His Word, which convicts our hearts and stirs us to repent, allowing Him to change us from the inside out.

It's important to keep in mind that, ultimately, the person who determines how much pruning takes place in your life is *you*. Ministers can preach the Word, and God will use that spoken Word to convict your heart. However, if you reject that conviction, the pruning will never happen and your life will still be hindered by those weights that keep you in a cycle of defeat.

Jesus died on the Cross and rose again so you could be an overcomer in every area of your life. But you have to be willing to let God prune you. Even though it may be uncomfortable, you should come to a point where you recognize and accept what God is doing because you know it is for your own good. This includes seeking out a church where the uncompromising Word is preached rather than settling for a watered-down Gospel that never challenges you.

There is something wrong with a church where people who live in sin regularly attend and yet still feel good about themselves. People who are living in sin should feel convicted when they go to church because of the Word that is being preached from the pulpit.

How about you, friend? Will you let God prune you? If your answer is no, then understand this: The sins and weights you keep in your life will be the hindrances that prevent you from enjoying God's best in life. On the other hand, a decision to walk in holiness and the fear of the Lord will cause you to walk in His abundance and bear much fruit for His glory!

CHAPTER SEVEN

How to See God

H oliness is a very serious matter to God. We can see just how serious it is to Him in Hebrews 12:14, which reads, *"Follow peace with all men, and holiness, without which no man shall see the Lord."*

God says that we won't see Him if we don't live holy lives. In other words, we won't see Him manifested in our lives on this earth or experience all His blessings. In fact, I'm convinced I know why many Christians aren't seeing His power manifested in their lives. The reason is simple: There are too many Christians who refuse to live holy lives.

God wants us to be a representation of His glory on the earth. He wants His glory to come into our churches, our homes, and our lives like never before. And God isn't the only One who wants to see His glory manifested. I'm constantly hearing ministers and laypeople alike declare that they want to see the glory of God fill their churches. People are hungering to see God move supernaturally in their midst. *So why isn't it happening?*

God isn't going to manifest His glory in our lives if we refuse even to begin the process of holiness that He requires. You see, when His glory came on the scene under the Old Covenant, it actually killed people if they were not holy. Now under the New Covenant, God's manifested glory won't kill us if we live unholy lives; instead, it just won't show up. We have to make adjustments in our lives if we want to see God, for His glory will not manifest in an unholy Church.

Get Rid of Pride!

I want to show you an excellent example in the Old Testament of how things can dramatically change when the necessary adjustments are made to allow the glory of God to come in.

ISAIAH 6:1,3

1 In the year that king Uzziah died I saw also the Lord sitting upon a throne, high and lifted up, and his train filled the temple.

3 And one [seraphim] cried unto another, and said, Holy, holy, holy, is the Lord of hosts: the whole earth is full of his glory.

In verse 1, we see that King Uzziah died. Then in verse 3, we read that the whole earth was filled with the glory of God.

One spiritual truth in these verses that we can apply to our lives today is that something has to "die" in us before we'll see God's glory. We have to desire to see His glory, no matter what the cost. We have to be willing to let go of *anything* that hinders His power from being manifested in our lives.

So what does King Uzziah represent to us today? Second Chronicles 26 gives us insight into the reason Uzziah's death was so important in allowing God's glory to fill the earth. Verse 1 tells us that he was crowned king of Judah. Let's go on to verses 4 and 5.

> 2 CHRONICLES 26:4,5
> 4   And [Uzziah] did that which was right in the sight of the Lord, according to all that his father Amaziah did.
> 5   And he sought God in the days of Zechariah, who had understanding in the visions of God: and as long as he sought the Lord, God made him to prosper.

Up to this point in his life, Uzziah seemed to be doing the right things, and God prospered him for his obedience. But later Uzziah made a critical mistake, referred to in Second Chronicles 26:16: *"But when he was strong, his heart was lifted up to his destruction: for he transgressed against the Lord his God, and went into the temple of the Lord to burn incense upon the altar of incense."*

The phrase "but when he was strong" is the key here. Uzziah became strong in his own eyes. He began to look around at his great kingdom and all the things he had accomplished, and he became proud. He had become so proud, in fact, that he actually went into the temple and burned incense on the altar. This was a blatant violation of God's instruction.

Thus, in Isaiah 6:1, Uzziah represents *pride*. And how does that translate to your personal walk with God? If you want to walk in holiness and see God's glory manifested in you and through you on a daily basis, *the first thing to put to death in your life is pride.*

'In You' Realities

Most Christians have heard of "in Him" or "in Christ" realities. There are many scriptures that tell us all that we are, all that we have, and all that we can do because we are *in Christ*. In fact, many books have been written to teach people about these verses and how to apply them in their lives.

However, there is another set of principles that is probably just as important as the "in Him" realities. I like to call them the *"in you"* realities! They're listed below, along with a corresponding scripture reference.

In and of yourself, you *are* nothing (Gal. 6:3).

In and of yourself, you *know* nothing (1 Cor. 8:2).

In and of yourself, you *have* nothing (1 Cor. 4:7).

In and of yourself, you *can do* nothing (John 15:5).

Can you imagine what would happen if Christians started meditating on how inadequate and powerless they are on their own? That would eliminate pride from their lives very quickly!

Successful businesspeople would no longer believe their businesses were built solely on their own talents and skills.

Ministers would no longer think it was their great personality and abilities that caused their ministries to grow.

Christians would begin to experience victory in their lives because they'd no longer rely on themselves to overcome the difficult circumstances they were facing.

Most importantly, believers would get themselves out of God's way so He could move and His glory could be manifested in their midst.

The Purpose of the Glory

Going back to Isaiah 6, we see that after Uzziah (the symbol of pride) dies, Isaiah sees the glory of God come into the temple in a vision. Then while still in God's Presence, Isaiah recognizes just how inferior he is to God: "*. . . Woe is me! for I am undone; because I am a* *man of unclean lips . . . for mine eyes have seen the King, the Lord of hosts"* (v. 5).

Verses 6 and 7 continue the account, relating how one of the seraphim takes a hot coal from the altar, lays it on Isaiah's lips, and purges his sin. Finally, verse 8 reveals why the manifestation of God's glory in our lives is so important: *"Also I heard the voice of the Lord, saying, Whom shall I send, and who will go for us? Then said I, Here am I; send me."*

The purpose of God's glory is not just to give us "goose bumps" or some interesting stories to tell other people. The glory of God *changes* us, first by causing us to recognize how awesome He is and then by purging sin from us. And all of this happens to accomplish God's ultimate goal for us—that we might be used by Him to accomplish His will on this earth.

It's All in Your Head

We keep talking about making adjustments in our lives, but where are those adjustments made? They are made *in our minds.* That is where holiness begins.

You see, our bodies don't just get into sin on their own. Our bodies don't decide to lust after another person or tell a lie on their own. All sin begins with a thought that goes unchecked. We have to *control* our thoughts; we have to refuse to allow our minds to do whatever they want to do.

Romans 12:1 reads, *"I beseech you therefore, brethren, by the mercies of God, that ye present your bodies a living sacrifice, holy, acceptable unto God . . . ."* We are to be *living* sacrifices, not dead ones! In the Old Testament, dead sacrifices were offered up to cover sin. But in the New Testament, we offer up our bodies as living sacrifices to be cleansed from sin. Our sin isn't just covered up—it is cleansed and washed away!

One of the first things you should do when you wake up every day is pray, "Father, I present my body a living sacrifice, holy and acceptable to You. I want You to use my body. I want You to think through my mind. I want You to do everything You want to do today through me and through my body."

Romans 12:2 continues, *"And be not conformed to this world: but be ye transformed by the renewing of your mind . . . ."* God tells us that we need to renew our minds and that when we do, we'll be transformed. The word "renew" in the Greek is where we get our English word "renovate." We need to renovate our thinking.

There is a television program called, "This Old House" that features people renovating old homes. These people always begin the actual process of renovation by first tearing out the things that don't belong in the reno-vated home they are working toward. In the same way, both Colossians 3:9 and Ephesians 4:22 instruct us to *put off* our old man. The Greek actually means to *strip off* the old man. We have to *strip off* our old ways of thinking and then obey God's instruction in Philippians 4:8.

> PHILIPPIANS 4:8
> 8 Finally, brethren, whatsoever things are true, whatsoever things are honest, whatsoever things are just, whatsoever things are pure, whatsoever things are lovely, whatsoever things are of good report; if there be any virtue, and if there be any praise, think on these things [occupy your mind with this].

Let's go back for a moment to Romans 12:2. The word "transform" is a Greek word from which we get the English word "metamorphosis," which means *a transformation that takes place through a process*. The best example we have of this is the way a caterpillar transforms into a butterfly. In the same way, our minds should constantly be getting transformed from "caterpillar thinking" (sinful thinking) into "butterfly thinking" (godly thinking).

Two Ways That God Changes Us

Renewing our minds leads to holiness, which allows us to see the glory of God in our lives. But how do we reach that first step of renewing our minds? One way is by reading the Word of God and letting it take root in our hearts.

James 1:25 reads, *"But whoso looketh into the perfect law of liberty, and continueth therein, he being not a forgetful hearer, but a doer of the work, this man shall be blessed in his deed."* That phrase "the perfect law of liberty" refers to the Word. God is saying that if you continue in the Word, you will be blessed. Why? Because the Word will change you, transforming you more and more into the person of holiness God created you to be.

The second way to renew your mind is found in Second Corinthians 3:18: *"But we all, with open face beholding as in a glass the glory of the Lord, are changed into the same image from glory to glory, even as by the Spirit of the Lord."* The word "changed" is the same Greek word translated as "transformed" in Romans 12:2. Thus, we see that our minds are also renewed by entering into the Presence, or the glory, of God through worship.

There will be times when you're in God's Presence, worshipping Him and telling Him how much you love Him, and suddenly He will say something like, "I saw how you treated that person. You have to ask him to forgive you and change your attitude toward him." What's happening? You're in a place where God can communicate to you and let you know about some areas in your life that aren't right. He's renovating you, changing you from a caterpillar into a butterfly!

So when God speaks to you about areas you need to change, don't get upset. Instead, get excited! Just know that He is leading you to a higher level of

fellowship and communion with Him where you will see
His glory manifested in your life!

CHAPTER EIGHT

The Wisdom of God

As you begin to study the fear of the Lord in the Bible, one of the things you quickly notice is how often wisdom and the fear of the Lord are mentioned together. In fact, Psalm 111:10 says, *"The fear of the Lord is the beginning of wisdom. . . ."* Once you begin to fear God and obey His commands, His wisdom will begin to operate in your life.

Today your marriage may be falling apart; your business may not be doing well; or your children may be giving you trouble. But if you will tap into the wisdom of God, you will never lack anything in life. Wisdom is one of the keys you need to carry out the plan of God for your life. It will put you on the road to success.

How Much Does Wisdom Cost?

One of the first things to know about wisdom is that it's free; it cannot be bought. Read carefully the following passage in Job.

JOB 28:12–19
12 But where shall wisdom be found? and where is the place of understanding?
13 Man knoweth not the price thereof; neither is it found in the land of the living.
14 The depth saith, It is not in me: and the sea saith, It is not with me.
15 It cannot be gotten for gold, neither shall silver be weighed for the price thereof.
16 It cannot be valued with the gold of Ophir, with the precious onyx, or the sapphire.
17 The gold and the crystal cannot equal it: and the exchange of it shall not be for jewels of fine gold.
18 No mention shall be made of coral, or of pearls: for the price of wisdom is above rubies.
19 The topaz of Ethiopia shall not equal it, neither shall it be valued with pure gold.

In the world's system of doing things, those who are the most beautiful, the most talented, the smartest, or the richest tend to have an advantage over everyone else. But that isn't the case in *God's* system. God doesn't favor one person over another. He says, "Whoever will serve Me and fear Me will receive My blessings"—and wisdom is one of the blessings He freely gives.

Some people have come to the conclusion that they are always "down on their luck" and that they won't ever amount to anything in life. One reason they may think that way is that they can never seem to make enough money to live the kind of life they desire to live. But God says to these people, "It doesn't matter how much money you have—all you need is *wisdom*. My wisdom will take care of everything else in your life."

God's message is the same to all of us: No matter what kind of circumstances we are facing in life, His wisdom is available to us, and we don't need money to buy it. That is *very* good news!

What Is Wisdom?

The Bible has a lot to say about knowledge, understanding, and wisdom, especially in the Book of Proverbs. In fact, these words are used together so often, people may think that they mean the same thing or that they're interchangeable. However, this isn't true, for each of them has a different meaning.

Most scholars agree that the definition of wisdom from the Hebrew language is *the ability to apply knowledge*. However, "understanding" is the middle step between knowledge and wisdom. First, we obtain knowledge; then we obtain understanding of that knowledge; and finally, we obtain wisdom, which is the ability to apply the knowledge we understand.

For example, if I were to watch a program on television that showed how an open-heart surgery is performed, I would gain knowledge about that subject, such as the steps that are taken in preparation for the procedure, during the procedure itself, and after the procedure. Nevertheless, you definitely wouldn't want me to perform the surgery on you! Why? Because I'd only possess some basic knowledge about the surgery.

But let's say that after watching the program, I become interested in open-heart surgery. I begin to do some research to learn more by reading medical books and journals on the subject. After a while, I actually begin to understand how and why different things are done in the procedure. But would you be willing to let me operate on you? I'm sure the answer would still be no, because although I have gained understanding of open-heart surgery, that still doesn't mean I can actually do it.

Now let's assume that after doing all that research, I decide to go to medical school to become a heart surgeon. My medical school training gives me the opportunity to actually witness several procedures firsthand and to assist the surgeons performing those procedures. Eventually, I begin to perform the procedures myself under the supervision of an experienced surgeon.

After several years of training, many hours spent in operating rooms, and many successful open-heart surgeries under my belt, would I finally meet the criteria you require? Do you think you'd be willing to let me operate on you? Your answer is much more likely to be yes at this point because I now possess wisdom regarding this subject. I can apply my knowledge of open-heart surgeries, coupled with my understanding of how to successfully complete the procedure.

Marriage is another example we can look at along this line. Some people have knowledge about marriage. They know what marriage is. Others have both knowledge and understanding regarding marriage. They not only know what it is, but they also know what it takes to make it successful. But God wants to give His people wisdom so they can then apply to their own lives the truths they know about marriage and start building successful marriages.

For example, if most Christians would stop and think about it, they'd agree that yelling at their spouses isn't the best way to handle a difficult situation. If they possessed God's wisdom, they'd remember that "a soft answer turneth away wrath" (Prov. 15:1) before they ever began to yell. As a result, they'd speak words of grace to their spouses that bring peace to the situation instead of strife.

The Wisdom of Proverbs

Of all the books in the Bible, Proverbs is probably one of the best ones to read to find God's wisdom. In fact, Proverbs 1 tells us that the very purpose Proverbs was written was to impart wisdom.

> PROVERBS 1:1–6 (*NIV*)
> 1 The proverbs of Solomon son of David, king of Israel:
> 2 for attaining wisdom and discipline; for understanding words of insight;
> 3 for acquiring a disciplined and prudent life, doing what is right and just and fair;
> 4 for giving prudence to the simple, knowledge and discretion to the young—
> 5 let the wise listen and add to their learning, and let the discerning get guidance—
> 6 for understanding proverbs and parables, the sayings and riddles of the wise.

First, Proverbs was written *to give us wisdom and discipline*. Discipline is one attribute that many people are lacking today. Unfortunately, that goes for the Church as much as for the world. For example, Christians think nothing of arriving to church fifteen, twenty, or even thirty minutes late. Many Christians don't even read their Bibles or pray on a regular basis. They live undisciplined lives. They can't even get to work on time. All of this is completely wrong according to the Word, for God wants His people to be disciplined.

Verse 4 tells us that another purpose for Proverbs is *to give prudence to simple people*. The word "simple" means *naïve* or *stupid*. God doesn't want us to be naïve.

Sometimes people will say about girls, "They're just naïve and gullible," as though those are cute little characteristics to have. But naïveté is not cute *or* right in God's eyes. In fact, naïveté can get girls into big trouble, especially with boys! The Book of Proverbs was actually written for the young Hebrew girls and boys of that day. It is obvious that God wanted to instill in them at a young age the ability *not to be stupid!*

Vine's gives the following definitions for the word prudence or prudent: "to have understanding"; "practical wisdom"; "quickness of apprehension"; and "the penetrating consideration which precedes action."[1] Considering these definitions, we know then that a prudent person will possess certain characteristics.

First, a prudent person will be careful in order to avoid mistakes. Imagine all the trouble and heartache people would avoid if they didn't make mistakes that cost them money or relationships! Businesspeople wouldn't put their money in bad investments. Husbands and wives wouldn't have affairs. People wouldn't get in over their heads with credit card debt.

Second, a prudent person is one who exercises sound judgment. Again, think how much better off we would be if we exercised sound judgment in the daily affairs of life!

Third, a prudent person manages carefully and with economy. Prudence that comes from God's wisdom will enable a person to manage his finances, his time, his home, or any other area of his life with economy—in other words, without wasting anything.

Finally, a prudent person will always know the best route to take and will always follow the most profitable source.

Wouldn't it be great if we always identified the most profitable source and then followed it? A prudent person exercising "practical wisdom" from God will do just that. God will show us where to put our money, who to enter into relationships with, and how to properly manage our time and our homes. All of these wonderful benefits, however, are contingent on our own diligence to pursue God's wisdom.

Characteristics of Wisdom

One of the things that's interesting about wisdom is that many times it's referred to in the Bible as a woman. For example, look at this passage of Scripture in Proverbs 3.

PROVERBS 3:13-15
13 Happy is the man that findeth wisdom, and the man that getteth understanding.
14 For the merchandise of it is better than the merchandise of silver, and the gain thereof than fine gold.
15 She is more precious than rubies: and all the things thou canst desire are not to be compared unto her.

Why is wisdom depicted as a female? I believe there are two reasons. First, just as with a woman, *wisdom must be pursued.* The way a man wins a wife is by pursuing a woman. He buys her flowers; he takes her out to dinner; he treats her the way she wants to be treated. Why does he do all that? Because women respond to how they are treated. If a man is kind, considerate, and loving toward a woman, she will probably act the same way toward him.

Wisdom is the same way. In Proverbs 8:17, wisdom is speaking and says, *"I love them that love me; and those that seek me early shall find me."* If you love wisdom, she will love you as well. But you have to actively go after her; she doesn't just come to you.

There is a second reason why wisdom is referred to as a female: *You have to maintain your relationship with wisdom in order to keep her.* After a man pursues a woman and marries her, he needs to maintain the relationship by continuing to treat her right. If he doesn't, that relationship will begin to collapse and eventually may even die.

We maintain our relationship with wisdom by continuing to fellowship with God and by faithfully spending time in His Word. However, just as some men are too busy working to spend time with their wives, sometimes we let ourselves get too busy to spend time with God and, as a result, stop receiving a continual supply of His wisdom. The truth is, if we only spend time with

God a couple of hours on Sunday, we won't obtain His wisdom for the situations we face on Monday through Saturday.

Proverbs 3:16 continues to speak about wisdom: *"Length of days is in her right hand; and in her left hand riches and honour."* Here's how it works: We choose to pursue wisdom as fervently as a man pursues a wife. We then strive to maintain our relationship with wisdom every day of our lives. In return, wisdom wraps her arms around us and gives us what is in her hands—long life, riches, and honor.

Verse 17 goes on to say, *"Her ways are ways of pleasantness, and all her paths are peace."* The word "peace" is the Hebrew word *shalom. Shalom* is an interesting word, for it also carries the meaning of *full* or *whole.* In Israel, it is used as a greeting. When people say, "Shalom," they are really asking, "Is everything okay? Do you have prosperity? Is everything in your life well?"

God's Word is therefore saying that if you get wisdom, nothing will be broken; nothing will be missing; and all will be well with you. That means you'll have total prosperity in your spirit, soul, and body. Every area of your life will prosper, including your marriage, your friendships, and your job.

Finally, let's look at what the next two verses say about wisdom:

PROVERBS 3:18,19

18 She is a tree of life to them that lay hold upon
her: and happy is every one that retaineth her.
19 The Lord by wisdom hath founded the earth; by
understanding hath he established the heavens.

Notice that God promises we'll be happy when we
have wisdom. His wisdom won't make us miserable or
bring evil things into our lives.

Verse 19 goes on to say that God created the whole
earth and everything in it by wisdom. He also created
you and me, so He knows exactly who we are and how
we function. By His wisdom, God knows what changes
we need in our lives, and He knows precisely what is
required for those changes to be effected in us.

The further we go in learning about wisdom, the
more we can see why God tells us, *"Wisdom is the prin-
cipal thing; therefore GET WISDOM . . ."* (Prov. 4:7)!

Witty Inventions

Proverbs 8 begins by painting a picture for us of
wisdom standing at the gates of the city, calling out to
those who are passing by. In verse 6, wisdom says,
*"Hear; for I will speak of excellent things; and the open-
ing of my lips shall be right things."* The phrase "right
things" in the Hebrew connotes *prosperity.* Thus, the
opening of wisdom's mouth brings prosperity.

In verses 10 and 11, the Bible again reiterates that it
is better to have wisdom than to have money: *"Receive*

my instruction, and not silver; and knowledge rather than choice gold. For wisdom is better than rubies; and all the things that may be desired are not to be compared to it."

The next verse gives us some insight as to why there is prosperity in wisdom's mouth and why it's better to have wisdom than money. Proverbs 8:12 reads, *"I wisdom dwell with prudence, and find out knowledge of witty inventions."*

Once again, we see that prudence and wisdom are linked together. But notice what God says in verse 12: that wisdom *". . . finds out knowledge of witty inventions."* If we will fear God and pursue His wisdom, He will give us witty inventions. And just one invention from God could literally bring millions, or even billions, of dollars into our hands!

You might ask, "What would someone do with that much money?" Well, here is one example: Years ago a man was sitting in a church service, listening to a missionary report on all the things he was doing in his ministry. That man was moved by what he heard and prayed, *Lord, if You gave me an invention, I would give ninety percent of the money to the church and to missions, and I'd live on only ten percent.*

Not long afterward, that man began a company that became a worldwide producer of earth-moving machinery. He became a billionaire and, as he had promised, gave ninety percent of his income to God and lived on only ten percent.

The key here is that the man's heart was right before God. He wanted the money so he could give into God's Kingdom. I'm convinced that God is looking for people like that. He wants to mightily bless people who fear Him, who seek His wisdom, and who want to be a blessing to others.

Concerning the link between wisdom and financial prosperity, we can also find a famous example in the Bible—King Solomon. First Kings 3 gives us the account of an exchange between Solomon and God soon after Solomon was crowned king.

God was so happy with Solomon that He told the young king He would give him whatever he asked. Solomon's answer pleased God greatly, for he asked for wisdom to judge, or to lead, God's people. The following is God's response to Solomon.

> 1 KINGS 3:11–13
> 11 And God said unto him, Because thou hast asked this thing, and hast not asked for thyself long life; neither hast asked riches for thyself, nor hast asked the life of thine enemies; but hast asked for thyself understanding to discern judgment;
> 12 Behold, I have done according to thy words: lo, I have given thee a wise and an understanding heart . . . .
> 13 And I have also given thee that which thou hast not asked, both riches, and honour: so that there

shall not be any among the kings like unto thee all thy days.

Solomon's request for wisdom instead of riches, honor, or long life pleased God so much that He gave Solomon wisdom *and* all those other blessings as well!

Let's go back to Proverbs 8 and look at two other verses that link wisdom and financial increase.

PROVERBS 8:20,21
20 I lead in the way of righteousness, in the midst of the paths of judgment:
21 That I may cause those that love me to inherit substance; and I will fill their treasures.

In modern language, the last part of verse 21 means, "I will fill their deposit" or "I will fill their bank account." God promises to fill our bank accounts if we get wisdom! That should make every one of us excited enough to dance!

You Can Have the Factory!

Scholars have studied Solomon's wealth and believe that he was worth eighty-nine billion dollars in that day's currency. Why was he able to acquire that kind of wealth? Because he decided to *take the factory*!

If someone offered to give you a nice car—a Cadillac, for example—you'd probably take it, right? Such a gift would probably be a great blessing to you. But what if someone offered to give you the General

Motors factory that produces the Cadillac? Which is the greater blessing? The factory is the greater blessing because it can continue to generate income and therefore continue to bless you.

Well, the wisdom of God is "the factory." If you go after wisdom, which is the "factory" where everything in God is produced, prosperity will be a continuous process in your life rather than something that just happens every now and then. God's wisdom contains everything you need. And if you pursue His wisdom, one day you'll look around at all the blessings in your life and wonder how you became so blessed. It won't happen overnight, but it *will* happen because that is what God's Word promises.

That's how Solomon became so wealthy. Someone didn't just come up to him one day and bless him with eighty-nine billion dollars. Solomon's enormous wealth was accumulated over time because wisdom kept bringing it into his life, and wisdom also showed him how to manage it.

Choosing to go after wisdom and take the factory is similar to the choice God put before the Israelites.

DEUTERONOMY 30:19
19 I call heaven and earth to record this day against
you, that I have set before you life and death,
blessing and cursing: therefore CHOOSE LIFE, that
both thou and thy seed may live.

The obvious correct choice for the Israelites was *life*. In the same way, the obvious choice for Christians today is to pursue wisdom and choose life. Yet there are actually Christians who choose death, and they'll even fight for the right to choose it!

Every time we refuse to believe what the Bible says about salvation, healing, prosperity, or anything else, we're choosing death. But we should all determine to fear God and go after wisdom so we can inherit the factory that produces abundant life!

---

[1] *Vine's Complete Expository Dictionary of Old and New Testament Words,* pp. 496-497.

CHAPTER NINE

How to Walk in the Wisdom of God

S o many times when we think of supernatural events, we think of healings and miracles. Certainly these *are* supernatural occurrences, but wisdom from God is also supernatural. Some people think wisdom is synonymous to common sense, but wisdom actually comes from Heaven. In fact, the Bible tells us in First Corinthians 1:30 that *Christ has been made wisdom* to us.

So if Christ lives in you in the Person of the Holy Spirit, He has already been made wisdom to you. You have all the wisdom you could ever need on the inside of you right now. All you have to do is tap into it!

Also, if we have attended church and heard the Word preached regularly for a period of time, we have stored a great amount of wisdom in our hearts; however, too often that wisdom just lies dormant in our lives. But if we ever learned to tap into the wisdom we already have, we'd begin to see our lives dramatically change for the better!

Sadly, though, many Christians are *not* tapping into the wisdom of God. That's obvious, because if they were really tapping into that wisdom, they would be the best at everything—the best husbands or wives, the best salespeople, the best plumbers, the best electricians, the best managers, the best assembly-line workers, etc. But so often, Christians are *not* the best in a given arena of life. In fact, in some workplace situations, Christians are known as the laziest workers in the company!

So if Christians have this wonderful wisdom available to them, why don't more of them use it? I believe the primary reason is that most Christians don't know *how* to access God's wisdom.

Understand the Source of Wisdom, And Then Go to the Source!

The first step in learning how to tap into God's wisdom is to understand where wisdom comes from. It's accurate to say that wisdom comes from God. But the Bible is more specific in pinpointing the source of wisdom and in telling us what we need to do to access it.

First, however, we need to understand the part *we* play in accessing divine wisdom.

106

PROVERBS 2:1,2

1   My son, if thou wilt receive my words, and hide
my commandments with thee;
2   So that thou incline thine ear unto wisdom, and
apply thine heart to understanding.

Notice the emphasis on what *we* have to do. It is
our responsibility to:

1. Receive God's words.

2. Hide His commandments in us.

3. Incline our ears to wisdom.

4. Apply our hearts to understanding.

In other words, we have to get ourselves in position
to access God's wisdom. Now let's look at the next few
verses to discover more about our role in tapping into
the wisdom of God.

PROVERBS 2:3-5

3   Yea, if thou criest after knowledge, and liftest
up thy voice for understanding;
4   If thou seekest her as silver, and searchest for
her as for hid treasures;
5   Then shalt thou understand the fear of the Lord,
and find the knowledge of God.

These verses tell us that we have to *desire* the Word
of God. The Word can't be something that we used to
love at one time but that we have ceased to hunger for
any longer. It doesn't matter if we've been saved for fifty
years and have read the Bible in its entirety five hundred
times—we should still hunger for God's Word! There will

always be more we can learn from it. Revelation from the Word of God can *never* be exhausted.

Now notice verse 6, which reads, *"For the Lord giveth wisdom: out of his mouth cometh knowledge and understanding."* Where does wisdom come from? *Out of the mouth of God.* What comes out of God's mouth? *Words.* And what is the Bible? *God's Word.*

So the wisdom that will teach you the fear of the Lord—which in turn will bring you long life, prosperity, healing, promotion, and all of God's other promises—comes from the Bible. If you search for wisdom in any other book, you will never find it.

The next step to accessing wisdom is found in Proverbs 2:10: *"When wisdom entereth into thine heart . . . ."* After wisdom comes out of the mouth of God, which is His Word, it then has to enter your heart.

It is at that point that you will begin to prosper and be exalted by God. All of a sudden you'll have the favor of God resting on you—and when the favor of God rests on you, *everything* begins to go right. New business comes your way. You receive a raise or a promotion at your job. Your relationship with your spouse and your children improves. You begin to find favor in *every* area of your life!

Operating in Wisdom

We have seen where God's wisdom comes from and the part we play in positioning ourselves to access it.

Now we can look at how to operate in the wisdom of God in our everyday lives.

> DEUTERONOMY 4:5,6
> 5 Behold, I have taught you statutes and judgments, even as the Lord my God commanded me, that ye should do so in the land whither ye go to possess it.
> 6 Keep therefore and do them; for this is your wisdom and your understanding in the sight of the nations . . . .

In these verses, Moses is speaking to the children of Israel. He tells them that their wisdom and understanding is to keep the commandments and to do them. This sounds a lot like James 1:22: *"But be ye doers of the word, and not hearers only, deceiving your own selves."*

One way to operate in wisdom is to hear the Word, accept the Word, and become a doer of what you hear. In other words, if you want to tap into God's wisdom, you can't just go to church and be blessed by the wonderful messages you hear without ever allowing those messages to change the way you live. *You have to apply to your life the truth that you hear.*

Another way to receive or access God's wisdom is to simply ask Him for it. James 1:5 says, *"If any of you lack wisdom, let him ask of God, that giveth to all men liberally, and upbraideth not; and it shall be given him."* This principle applies to every area of life. You might be at work one day and think, *I need wisdom to handle this situation.* Just ask God, and immediately He will begin to impart the wisdom you need to come through that situation with the best possible result.

This is especially important in marriages. We're constantly hearing about the great differences between men and women. Both genders seem to think differently, function differently, and perceive situations differently.

So how can you understand your spouse? Ask God for wisdom. Who better to ask for help than the One who created both of you?

The problem with some Christians is that they always want to ask other people, including their pastors, for advice on how to handle a situation. But *God* should be the first One they turn to. Even pastors, who are there to help their church members, don't always have all the answers.

James 1:5 is a great verse, but we also have to read the first part of verse 6 in order to put it in the proper context: *"But let him ask in faith, nothing wavering . . . ."* This is the key to asking for wisdom. You can't receive anything from God unless you are asking in *faith.*

That's why this verse doesn't say we're to *beg* for wisdom. Our prayers won't work if we're only praying, "Please, God, give me wisdom! I just have to have wisdom!"

Instead, we are to ask in faith, confident that God's Word says He will perform what He has promised us.

God wants us to pray, "Father, I need wisdom, and I ask You for it in Jesus' Name. I believe I receive wisdom for my situation, and I thank You for it!" Then whenever we think about the situation throughout the day, we should thank God that He has given us the wisdom we have requested.

On the other hand, if you begin to doubt whether or not you'll receive the wisdom you need after you have prayed, you are the person whom James describes in the next few verses.

JAMES 1:6-8
6 . . . For he that wavereth is like a wave of the sea driven with the wind and tossed.
7 For let not that man think that he shall receive any thing of the Lord.
8 A double minded man is unstable in all his ways.

We're unstable if we keep asking God again and again for the wisdom He has already promised us. God expects us to become stable people of faith by taking Him at His Word and simply believing that if He says He'll give us wisdom, *it will happen*!

Wisdom and the Word

I've already briefly touched on the next factor in receiving wisdom: *We have to get into God's Word.* This goes back to the necessity of hungering for the truth in the Word, for God must have something in us to work with. We shouldn't expect to receive God's wisdom if we don't spend time alone with Him—praying, worshipping, and reading His Word.

Look at what Paul says about the connection between wisdom and the Word in the following verses.

EPHESIANS 1:15–17
15 Wherefore I also, after I heard of your faith in the Lord Jesus, and love unto all the saints,
16 Cease not to give thanks for you, making mention of you in my prayers;
17 That the God of our Lord Jesus Christ, the Father of glory, may give unto you the spirit of wisdom and revelation in the knowledge of him.

We can see from this passage of Scripture that 1) there is a spirit of wisdom, and 2) we can ask God for wisdom both for ourselves and for other people. But notice again how important the Word is in receiving this wisdom.

The last part of this passage talks about the spirit of "revelation in the knowledge of Him." The knowledge of God is contained in His Word, and revelation comes as we study and meditate on the Bible. Therefore, it would do us well to look at an example of how God's wisdom and His Word are integrally linked together.

Let's say a married man who fears God and spends time in His Word asks for wisdom regarding his marriage. One day he's reading his Bible and comes across Ephesians 5:25, which commands him to love his wife as Christ loved the Church, even to the point of giving himself for her. Then a few days later, the husband reads Romans 5, and God shows him in verse 8 that Christ loved him and died for him while he was still a sinner.

Suddenly the Holy Spirit puts the two verses together for the husband, and he realizes that he needs to start loving his wife like she's the most important person in the world, even to the point of laying down his life for her. At that moment, wisdom is operating in that man's life. Will that wisdom change his marriage for the better? If he becomes a doer of it, you bet it will!

Now suppose that the man's wife, who also fears the Lord, begins to ask God for wisdom regarding her marriage as well. One day as she is spending time in the Word, the wife comes across Ephesians 5:22, which commands her to submit to her husband. Then a few days later, she reads God's command in First Peter 3:5 and 6 for her to be in subjection to her husband the way Sarah was to Abraham.

God begins to deal with this wife's heart. Suddenly the Holy Spirit shows her that she hasn't been recognizing her husband as the leader of their home, and she begins to make some adjustments on the inside to change that. What happened? God was able to take her knowledge of the Word and show her how to apply it to her marriage. Wisdom is now operating in that woman's life. Will it change her marriage for the better? You bet!

What happened in these two examples? The first part of Ephesians 1:18 was activated in the lives of this husband and wife: *"The eyes of your understanding being enlightened* [flooded with light] . . . ."* God turned on the light in the hearts of this couple because *they asked in faith for wisdom.*

The wisdom of God is so simple. All you have to do is ask for it in faith. So every day when you first wake up, ask God for the spirit of wisdom and revelation. Ask Him to open the eyes of your understanding.

As you do, the divine wisdom that begins to change your life will impact those around you as well. It will cause you to be ready when someone asks you why you have such a great marriage or how you're able to do so well on your job. You'll go right through that open door of opportunity to tell that person about Jesus and what He's done for you!

CHAPTER TEN

Reverencing God

W e know that to fear the Lord means to have a wholesome dread of ever displeasing Him. But there is another side to fearing the Lord, and that involves *reverence*. Reverence for God should be something every Christian practices every day of their lives.

Reverencing God simply means acknowledging that He is in you everywhere you go. That attitude of awareness will keep you in a position for God to continually move through you in every situation of life.

You Are a Carrier of God!

Because people don't stay in fellowship with God all the time, they feel like they have to "work up" to God to get Him to move on their behalf. But God doesn't need us to make Him willing to move in our lives. He's *always* ready and willing to show His power on our behalf. The problem lies with us. We don't realize that we are carriers of God because we forget that He is always with us.

An excellent example of this powerful truth is a great man of God who lived during the first part of the twentieth century. Sometimes when this man stepped onto a train to travel somewhere and the people on the train saw him, they would immediately fall to their knees and begin repenting of their sins!

Why did that happen? *Because this minister never lost sight of the fact that he was a carrier of God.* God's Presence in his life eventually became so strong that people were convicted of their sins just by being around him.

Now, all Christians are carriers of God, but not all Christians reveal His Presence in their lives. You see, each believer plays a part in how strong God's Presence is in him. That is where reverence comes in.

Reverence is actually just another word for the fear of the Lord. Again, it means carrying God everywhere you go and acknowledging that He is in you. This puts you in a position to always be ready to be used by Him.

There are many places in the Bible that talk about the fact that God lives in us. First Corinthians 3:16 is a key scripture along this line: *"Know ye not that ye are the temple of God, and that the Spirit of God dwelleth in you?"* As we reverence God, this awareness of the Holy Spirit's indwelling Presence begins to affect every area of our lives.

Many Christians put on a good act when they're around other people. They act like they're super-spiritual men or women of faith, but behind closed doors, they're involved in all kinds of sin. These people mistakenly think that as long as no one sees or knows what they do, they'll be okay. But they can only live a lie before other people as long as they don't acknowledge God's constant Presence in their lives. Once they start acknowledging God, they'll begin to avoid doing anything that would displease Him. Why? Because they'll finally understand that God Himself is both with them and in them everywhere they go.

Too many Christians are people-pleasers. It's more important to them what their pastor and Christian friends think about them than what *God* thinks. But in the end, God is the only One who matters, and reverencing Him is the key to bringing about a true change in attitude.

How to 'Practice the Presence of God'

Hebrews 12:28 reads, *"Wherefore we receiving a kingdom which cannot be moved, let us have grace, whereby we may serve God acceptably with reverence and godly fear."* We see here that reverence is tied to godly fear. We can't reverence the Lord without fearing

Him, and we can't fear the Lord if we don't reverence Him. The important question, then, is how *do* we reverence God?

The way you reverence God is by doing what some people have called "practicing the Presence of God." This simply means that you always acknowledge God in you. As you do that, you'll begin to recognize God's Presence in your life more and more.

I've had the privilege of meeting and being in the presence of some great men and women of God. One thing I've noticed about all these individuals is that they're always conscious of God in them. In fact, many times I've heard them quietly speak praises to God. For example, they may be sitting in a restaurant having dinner with a group of people, but under their breath, they're saying, "Praise the Name of Jesus." They don't speak loudly so that everyone else can hear it; they just say it quietly to themselves.

What are these people doing? *They are practicing the Presence of God.* This is what keeps God's power activated in their lives so it can be manifested through them to help other people.

But something else happens in a person's life who continually practices the Presence of God. Look at what Hebrews 12:29 says: *"For our God is a consuming fire."* Just as a fire burns up and consumes everything in its path, God burns up sin in the lives of those who yield themselves to Him.

You see, once a Christian begins to fear and reverence God, sin begins to lose its grip in that person's life. For example, perhaps the person has struggled with pornography in the past. But as he makes a practice of acknowledging God in his life day by day, he soon discovers that he no longer struggles with the sinful desires he once had, for his new awareness of God has set him free!

The key is to be consumed with God and His Presence—to keep uppermost in your heart and mind the awareness that He is with you and in you. Make it a practice to acknowledge Him everywhere you go and in everything you do. Acknowledge Him while you're watching television; while you're getting ready for work; while you're sitting in a business meeting; while you're repairing your car; or while you're buying groceries. Acknowledge God in *everything* that you do. I assure you that this *can* be done; it just takes a quality decision to start practicing His Presence.

As you do this, you'll become sensitive to God and begin to hear His voice more clearly. This will allow God to lead and direct you throughout each day. And keep in mind—this is *not* just for ministers. It's for every believer, including you!

Keep Your Thoughts Fixed on God

Malachi 3:16 talks about the kind of people who are consumed with God and who covet His Presence in their lives. It says, *"Then they that feared the Lord spake often one to another: and the Lord hearkened, and heard it, and a book of remembrance was written before him for them that feared the Lord, and that thought upon his name."*

The people in this verse feared the Lord and thought on His Name. Isn't that refreshing? Instead of thinking about their problems and all the bad things the devil was doing to them, they thought about *God*.

That is a key to practicing the Presence of God. You must keep your thoughts on Him and not allow your mind to run wild and dwell on all sorts of ungodly things.

As you begin to acknowledge God in you and continually meditate on His Word, His Presence will fill you up and accompany you wherever you go. You'll walk into a room, and people will know there is something different about you as they sense God's Presence. You'll carry yourself a certain way because you know Jesus, the King of kings and the Lord of lords, and because you're aware that the God who spoke the universe into existence lives within you and is shining out of you.

Paul talked several times about the importance of keeping our minds fixed on the things of God. For example, in Philippians 4:8, he wrote, *"Finally, brethren, whatsoever things are true, whatsoever things are honest, whatsoever things are just, whatsoever things are pure, whatsoever things are lovely, whatsoever things are of good report; if there be any virtue, and if there be any praise, think on these things."*

What was Paul talking about here? Practicing the Presence of God by keeping our thoughts fixed on godly things. Also, in Colossians 3:1 and 2, we're commanded to *". . . seek those things which are above, where Christ sitteth on the right hand of God. Set your affection on things above, not on things on the earth."* Again, God is telling us to keep our minds on Him and on heavenly things. We're not supposed to get all wrapped up in the things of this world.

First John 2:15 reiterates this point: *"Love not the world, neither the things that are in the world . . . ."* But then John takes it a step further: *". . . If any man love the world, the love of the Father is not in him."*

You have to have the mindset that says, "I love life, and there are things on this earth that I enjoy, but I'm just passing through. I'm not going to love this world or the things in it more than I love God." You can maintain that mindset as long as you keep your mind on God.

If believers could only get hold of this truth! It is so simple and yet so life-changing!

No matter where you go or what you're doing—morning, day, and night—think about God. Talk to God and about God as much as possible. If you want to see signs, wonders, and miracles manifested in your life, this is one of the keys. God will begin to move supernaturally on your behalf as you keep your thoughts fixed on Him.

Allow God to Direct Your Life

Proverbs 3:5 and 6 is a familiar passage of Scripture for most Christians, but let's look at it from a different perspective. It reads, *"Trust in the Lord with all thine heart; and lean not unto thine own understanding. In all thy ways acknowledge him, and he shall direct thy paths."*

Verse 6 tells us that if we acknowledge God, He will direct us. In the past, we may have read this verse and thought it was talking about acknowledging God whenever we make a decision or do something important in our lives. But it's actually talking about acknowledging God every time we take a breath—with every part of our being, day and night, all the time.

This is the actual message of this verse: "Trust in the Lord with all your heart, and don't lean on your own understanding. In all your ways—every time you take a breath—acknowledge Him, and He will direct your life."

If we truly want God to direct our paths, we need to continually recognize the fact that God is living in us. Instead of "stopping to smell the roses," we should stop to acknowledge the presence of God!

The last part of verse 6 says, " . . . *He shall direct thy paths."* The Hebrew says He will not only direct your paths, but, He will make your paths straight and show you what road to take.[1]

There are certain things God wants us to do, and He will lead us in those areas—but it all begins with acknowledging Him. That is the human part in this equation. God's part is to direct our paths. And as we do our part, God will be faithful to do His.

Make Your Faith Operative!

In the Book of Philemon, Paul expands on this idea of acknowledging God by showing us how it relates to faith. Verse 6 reads, *"That the communication of thy faith may become effectual by the acknowledging of every good thing which is in you in Christ Jesus."* That word "effectual" means *operative* or *active*.

There's a principle here that says when a person acknowledges that Christ is in him, he makes his faith operative. This explains why so many Christians have faith that isn't operative—because they don't acknowledge who is in them!

Think about it. If you were to go through each day continually reminding yourself that the Creator of Heaven and earth is in you, there isn't anything you could face that would look too big or too difficult. Your faith would be operative, and your attitude would change toward all the things the devil throws your way. You'd start thinking, *Devil, you messed with the wrong person—not because of who I am, but because I have*

Christ in me. So look out, devil! I have the victory over you!

How Close Will You Get to God?

God wants us to acknowledge Him all the time so He can work in and through us. However, He will never force Himself on us. As James 4:8 tells us, *"Draw nigh [close] to God, and he will draw nigh [close] to you."*

When we talk about practicing the Presence of God and acknowledging God in us, it's important to understand that God will only get as close to us as we want Him to. If we want to live in close fellowship with God, we need to start drawing nearer to Him. As we do, He will draw closer to us. On the other hand, if we decide that we want God to stand far off from us, He'll do it. In other words, God will match our actions and give us as much of Him as we want.

How does this principle work in your everyday life? When you wake up on a Monday morning and your flesh wants to dominate your day with a bad attitude, you have a choice to make. You can allow your flesh to rule you and keep you in a bad mood all day, or you can start your day by acknowledging God.

So begin your day by talking to Him. For instance, you could say, "Father, good morning. I'm ready to go today. I acknowledge that You live on the inside of me." What happens when you do that? It allows God to become active in you and to change the way your day is going for the better. Instead of your being mean to everyone you meet that day, God will work through you and cause you to see manifestations of His glory!

Always keep in mind what James 4:8 says: If we'll come close to God, He'll come close to us. Sometimes the devil convinces us that God doesn't want to be around us. But remember what happened way back in the Garden of Eden. Adam was the one who ran from God in the Garden when God came looking for him. God has always wanted to have a relationship with mankind. We are the ones who run from *Him*.

Practice His Presence And Get the Victory!

Now let's see how this all ties together. The fear of the Lord is to hate evil. Well, if you're acknowledging God, you won't do evil things. When temptation comes, you'll say, "No, I'm going to choose the right direction and the right road because God Himself lives in me, and I don't want to displease Him." But when you're *not* acknowledging God, you'll easily fall into sin because pleasing Him is not on your mind.

Here's a scenario you're probably familiar with: You hear a message on a Sunday morning about overcoming sin, and you get excited about going out and winning the victory. But by Thursday or Friday, you've fallen right back into the sin you were supposed to overcome.

What is the worst thing you could do at that point? *Allow yourself to get discouraged and give up.*

You have to understand that as you continue to acknowledge God, you're being strengthened on the inside no matter *how* many times you may fail. Just be patient and keep acknowledging God's Presence in your life. Before you know it, the sin that always used to take you down won't even be a temptation to you. You'll have the strength to say no to it.

That's what it takes to be an overcomer and to enjoy success in this life. It's really very simple. You just have to learn to say *no* to the devil's temptations. Fortunately, that becomes easier and easier to do as you fear God and acknowledge the Greater One living on the inside of you!

The stakes couldn't be higher, friend, for whether or not you walk in the fear of God is a decision that will determine the outcome of your life. So what kind of harvest do you choose to reap? An unending cycle of unanswered prayer and chronic defeat? Or an upward climb toward prosperity and success as you walk through each day in the fear of the Lord?

---

[1] Ibid., p. 170.

"How Do I Get to Heaven?"

The Bible declares that we can know that we have eternal life. I John 5:13 reads, *"These things have I written unto you that believe on the name of the Son of God; that ye may know that ye have eternal life, and that ye may believe on the name of the Son of God."*

Acts 2:21 tells us that, *". . . whosoever shall call on the name of the Lord shall be saved."* And Romans 10:9,10 (NKJV) reads, *"That if you confess with your mouth the Lord Jesus, and believe in your heart that God has raised Him from the dead, you will be saved. For with the heart one believes to righteousness; and with the mouth confession is made to salvation."*

Laying hold on eternal life is as simple as believing that Jesus Christ is the Son of God, that He died and was raised from the dead, and then confessing (or saying) that with your mouth. If you have never called on the Name of the Lord—don't put it off one more day. The following is a prayer of salvation. Read aloud this prayer and receive eternal salvation!

Prayer of Salvation

"Heavenly Father, I come to you in Jesus' Name. The Bible says that if I call on the name of the Lord, I will be saved. So, I do that now. I believe in my heart that Jesus came to the earth, was crucified, and rose from the dead. I confess that Jesus is Lord. I thank you that I am now a Christian—a child of God! I am saved and have received eternal life."

If you just prayed this prayer out loud, the Bible says you have instantly become a new creature in Christ: *"old things have passed away, behold all things are new"* (2 Cor. 5:17). You will never be the same. Now you need to find a good local church and get involved as part of the family of God. Find a church that will love and care for you, and teach you the Word of God.

About the Author

M ichael Cameneti, Senior Pastor of Canton Christian Fellowship, Canton, Ohio, is an anointed teacher of the Word of God known for boldly proclaiming the goodness, faithfulness, and mercy of God. Pastor Mike is passionate about winning the lost to Christ. The very drive of his heart is to "go into all the world and preach the Gospel to every creature" (Mark 16:15).

Today, many believers stand together with Pastor Mike and his wife, Barb, as God continues to direct and guide each phase of ministry at Canton Christian Fellowship.

To contact the author, write:
Mike Cameneti
P.O. Box 35309
Canton, Ohio 44735
or visit www.ccfchurch.com

Michael Cameneti

Additional teachings from *this author*

To Order: Visit our website at **www.ccfchurch.com** or call **1-888-872-4991**.

If you enjoyed this book, you'll want to get the entire teaching series on audio cassette!

The Missing Ingredient to Success

Pastor Michael Cameneti

Why do so many Christians seem to struggle from one defeat to the next, never really experiencing the abundant life God has for them? The answer is no mystery, it is declared clearly by God Himself throughout His Word: *The missing ingredient is the fear of the Lord.*

Part 1 (6 tapes) **$24⁰⁰** #1140-1
Part 2 (4 tapes) **$16⁰⁰** #1140-2

Healing Made Simple

Pastor Michael Cameneti

It is God's will for His people to walk in divine health every day of their lives; He has promised healing in His Word. In this book, you'll learn where sickness comes from, the benefits included in God's plan of redemption, and the power of Christ in you. With powerful revelation from the Word of God and straight-forward delivery, Pastor Mike imparts "Healing Made Simple."

Paperback **$12⁰⁰** #336-01

Keys to Victorious Living

Pastor Michael Cameneti

God's plan for you includes a life of victory. Regardless of your circumstances or how many times you may have tried and failed to succeed, God calls you an overcomer. He has given you the keys in His Word to unlock everything you need from heaven to enjoy victorious living.

Paperback **$10⁹⁹** #336-02

Home Improvement

Pastor Michael Cameneti

Statistics show that in the world today, 50% of marriages end in divorce. With this staggering figure, we need to examine the blueprint for building and maintaining a strong marriage and family. In this series, Pastor Michael Cameneti examines the basic building blocks needed for structuring a solid family and home.

8-tape audio series **$32⁰⁰** #1144 • 8-CDs **$40⁰⁰** #3-1144

About
Canton Christian Fellowship™

A Church to Call Home™

Pastors Michael &
Barbara Cameneti

Pastors Mike and Barb Cameneti, under the direction of the Holy Spirit, established Canton Christian Fellowship in the winter of 1988. Today, CCF has grown into a large, diverse, and multi-faceted ministry, impacting people of all ages In our community and beyond. Sensitive to the leading of the Holy Spirit, Pastors Mike and Barb boldly minister the uncompromised Word of God clearly and accurately, with the gifts of the Spirit accompanyIng the preaching of the Word.

It is our desire to provide an environment where you and your family will experience the goodness of God and His abounding love toward you. If you do not have a home church and live in the Canton area, we invite you to be a part of our church family. At Canton Christian Fellowship, we're "A Church to Call Home."

Pastor Mike can also be seen on our *Keys to Victorious Living™* television broadcast every week. Check our website for program listings.

Contact Information:
PO Box 35309 • Canton, Ohio 44735
www.ccfchurch.com • 330-492-0925

RHEMA
Bible Training Center

Want to reach the height of your potential?

RHEMA can take you there.

- proven instructors
- alumni benefits
- career placement
- hands-on experience
- curriculum you can use

Do you desire—

- to find and effectively fulfill God's plan for your life?
- to know how to "rightly divide the Word of truth"?
- to learn how to follow and flow with the Spirit of God?
- to run your God-given race with excellence and integrity?
- to become not only a laborer but a *skilled* laborer?

If so, then RHEMA Bible Training Center is here for you!

For a free video and full-color catalog, call:
1-888-28-FAITH—Offer #4177
(1-888-283-2484)
www.rbtc.org

RHEMA Bible Training Center admits students of any race, color, or ethnic origin.

Word of Faith

The *Word of Faith* is a full-color magazine with faith-building teaching articles by Rev. Kenneth E. Hagin and Rev. Kenneth Hagin Jr.

The Word of Faith also includes encouraging true-life stories of Christians overcoming circumstances through God's Word, and information on the various outreaches of Kenneth Hagin Ministries and RHEMA Bible Church.

To receive a free subscription to *The Word of Faith*, call:
1-888-28-FAITH—Offer #4178
(1-888-283-2484)
www.rhema.org/wof

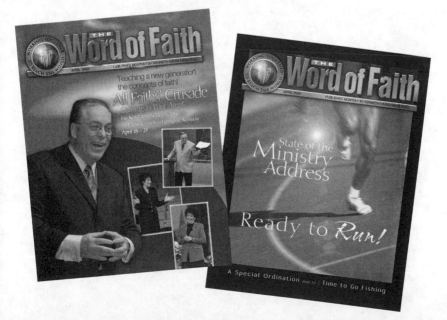